Wrinkled but Not Ruined

Counsel for the Elderly

Jay E. Adams

TIMELESS TEXTS
Woodruff, SC

Contents

Preface

As I write this book I am approaching my 70th birthday. I find that I am still able to think clearly and, I hope, to write helpfully. I plan to do both. Age 70 is neither too old nor too young to consider seriously the remaining days that may lie before me. They may be many or few, but they do call for a sort of evaluation of my life in the light of the past and the possible future. "Oh my," you say, "he's going to reminisce and speak sentimentally about the years to come. Perhaps I'd better lay this book aside right now." Wait a second, please! *This is a book about ministering to others*, not merely about age—and, especially, not about me.

I am speaking about myself only because I think that letting you know that I am growing older, from one point of view, qualifies me to write about counseling older folks. I am facing many of the problems that older people face,[1] and I think that I may reflect upon some of these things illustratively. But please understand (I'll say it once more) this is *definitely not* a book about me or about old age in general. It is a book about *ministering or counseling to those who are getting older.*

You may have a different definition of old age than I. I think that I should give you mine. Old age can be considered two ways: *chronologically* or *functionally.* Those who determine that at a certain point in time they will reach old age (65, 70, or whatever) set up an arbitrary milepost. I am not at all convinced that is the only way that we should look at old age. I would prefer to consider it from a functional point of view. I am not sure that

---

[1] So far, in addition to the usual aches and pains that one experiences as he grows older, I have suffered from atrial fibrillation, arthritic problems, cataracts leading to lens implants, and a menengioma, all of which are more or less under control at the moment.

everyone becomes "old" at the same time. I have known some who seem old at the age of 30 and others who act young at the age of 70. Moreover, age is, on the one hand, a matter of a body's aging; on the other hand it is a matter of one's attitude remaining youthful or aging. Until now there has been little that could be done about keeping the body cells from aging (though in the last few months there have been news reports about scientists in Texas who claim to have found the reason cells age and are now taking measures to stop the process; we shall see!). But, so long as one has the physical capacity to do so (that is, his brain is still fairly well intact[1]), he may *choose* to consider himself old or young and think and act accordingly.[2] Admittedly, he may not be as spry as he was in the past, but there are other ways in which a buoyant spirit, bent on serving the Lord, may manifest itself in youthful attitudes.

At any rate, as I am growing older in body, I think that it is incumbent upon me to leave something of a heritage to my fellow counselors about the matter of helping those both older in body and in spirit. It is not as if the Bible had nothing to say about the matter. Indeed, as I trust you will see, there is much in the Scriptures about old age and God's view of it. That means that there is significant material for counselors to contemplate. I hope that younger counselors will be able to think with me about these matters and thereby find themselves better able to help those of us who are entering "old age" (however determined).

I will never forget several years ago when I decided to purchase a year's pass to the Wild Animal Park outside of Escondido, California (where I lived at that time). The young lady seated behind the window inquired, "Senior Citizen?" Those

---

[1] The brain is not the spirit; the two must not be confused. The brain, along with everything else that is placed in the ground at death and rots, is a part of the body.

[2] When someone says, "My, you look good [young] for your age," you may take it that he thinks you're old!

words stopped me in my tracks! No one had ever asked me that before. I had never thought of myself that way. It didn't take me long to recover, however, when I realized that there would be a significant "rake off" for a Senior, so I asked her, "At what age is a person classified as such?" When she told me I realized that, sure enough, I qualified for a substantial discount. Ever since, I have enjoyed cashing in on similar "senior" privileges at restaurants, motels, and the like. When I moved to South Carolina, because of my age, the state even gave me a lifetime hunting/fishing license gratis! So, not everything about age is downhill. Biblically, in fact, we soon shall see that there is much that ought to be thought of as positive about aging. We must discover God's perspective and how to help others to get in line with it.

Well, ever since I experienced that minor jolt at the Wild Animal Park, I have paid much closer attention to the matter of age than ever before. That experience set off in me a new line of thinking about myself (and others who are in the same boat). I admit that this jolt was but a very mild example when compared to the many larger jolts that some persons encounter as they grow older—many of which the outcomes are not nearly so pleasant. It is these matters to which the biblical counselor must address himself. I hope to write helpfully to enable him to do so. At present, my problems due to age are meager compared to many others of my age. But, lack of energy, failing health and other difficulties have already either come upon me to some extent or, I must realize, possibly lie right around the corner. I have experienced some of the firstfruits of aging already.

I confess, also, that while my focus throughout will be on counseling older people, I intend to make such personal applications of the biblical data as I am able. As I garner promises (an important factor), principles, and practices from the Scriptures, I shall also be preparing myself for much that (if I live that long) seems inevitable. As I want to reemphasize it, this is a book about ministering to others, first and foremost. But I hope, as well, that it is a book that elderly persons themselves may find profitable in meeting problems God's way on their own—apart from counseling. For them, it should not be so difficult simply to turn around what is said to counselors and apply God's Word to themselves.

Introduction

Counseling the elderly is both the same and very different from counseling anyone else. That is to say, fundamental biblical principles persist regardless of a person's age. Throughout life they do not change. Old age, *per se*, lets no one off the hook. God does not relax or alter His commandments when one reaches a certain age. But as a person ages, the problems he encounters are added to those with which he has contended since youth.[1] These additional burdens may tend to exacerbate and intensify those lifelong difficulties, particularly if one has never come to grips with the latter God's way. It is difficult to make changes that one ought to have made many years before.[2] Moreover, biblical principles learned earlier must now be applied to new circumstances. This is one of the reasons why "change" seems so hard to many.[3] It is, therefore, important for biblical counselors to understand the sorts of things that are new while, at the same time, maintaining principles that are old. Because I have written little about such matters before, it is my desire to do so in this book.

For the first time in history, we who are over 60 years of age constitute a significant portion of the population. At the beginning of the century, the average life expectancy was 47 years. Now, at the end of this century, that figure will escalate to 80 years—nearly double! People's maximum lifetimes aren't much longer (virtually no one lives beyond 120 years of age); the difference is that so many more reach the upper limits. Those sup-

---

[1] It is also true that some burdens are lifted (earning a living, manual labor he is no longer capable of performing, etc.).

[2] But by no means impossible.

[3] Especially when so many changes may come all at once. That can seem overwhelming.

posedly long-lived Russians, for example, who were said to be dying in great numbers at ages well over 100, it was discovered, forged their birth certificates in order to avoid the draft in World War I. However, the human body, unencumbered by disease, should last from 115-120 years. Conceivably, while the upper limits remain constant, greater success in eliminating disease may mean that even more may reach these ripe old ages![1]

Barring accidents, widespread riots, terrorism, deadly epidemics and war, today a 65-year-old man, on average, may look forward to living at least 15 more years, a 65-year-old woman 19 more years. If present trends continue, the number of people over 65 will *double* to about 60 million by the year 2020 AD. The problems, challenges and opportunities of old age increasingly will be with us whether we like it or not and will present us with the additional need for counseling older persons. This is something that no biblical counselor should be unaware of. He is going to have a *load* of such counseling in the very near future.[2] The nature of the counseling challenge will change.

It is, therefore, incumbent upon counselors to know what is involved in old age, what God has to say about it, and how to counsel the elderly in a biblical way. For instance, ask yourself what you know about aging. Do you tend to avoid older counselees or give them short shrift? Are you nonplussed when you absolutely *must* deal with them? Do you have other problems along these lines? If you must answer any, or all, of these questions in the affirmative, you need to think more deeply about what God says concerning growing old and how He expects you to help those who are doing so. I urge you to spend the necessary time and energy to consider the matter in depth.

---

[1] For facts about this, see "Health," *The Washington Post*, April 14, 1987, p. 14.
[2] Not to speak of the fact that he will be entering into old age himself!

Chapter One

What Is Aging?

This question may be answered several ways. You may, for instance, think of it in terms of physical deterioration alone, as many do, or you may take a broader perspective that includes elements beyond the physical, as I intend to do in this book. I suggest that we think of aging as **a process of loss.**[1]

These elements of loss have been occasioned by the fall and the curse that followed it. It is a process that, in accordance with God's curse, leads to death. Aging is clearly a matter of man's present mortality. When God warned that in the day man would eat of the tree of the knowledge of good and evil he would **surely die** He meant just that (cf. Genesis 2:17; 3:19). Spiritually speaking, man did die in the sense that he was separated from God—in body and spirit. He also began the process of dying physically—the separation of the body from the spirit. And ultimately, if he fails to trust Christ as his Savior in this life, in the life to come he will die eternally—as his body and his spirit will be separated from God forever. Death came with the fall of man into sin as part of the curse. Aging, as loss, began then and there in the garden of Eden.

Paul speaks of aging in terms of **decaying** (II Corinthians 4:16), and calls the present aging body a **humiliated** body (Philippians 3:21). Man *lost* his original state of perfection and his communication with God. There is no doubt that the deterioration of the physical body itself, being a humiliation to the man

---

[1] Not that there are no gains to be realized in the process, but it is the loss factor that occasions most of the needs for counseling.

who once had dominion over the earth (but *lost* it) has dimensions that extend far beyond the fact that physical limitations usually come with age. It is also the effect of these limitations, pains, and diseases upon the persons who, because of Adam's sin, are suffering the humiliating punishment for it, with which we as counselors must contend. There are dimensions even beyond that—the greatest loss of all was the loss of communion with God and walking in the cool of the day.[1]

Sin's curse, leading to these huge losses, has brought with it frustration and bondage (cf. Romans 8:20ff.) and their consequences, **suffering and groaning** (8:18, 23); these losses are often exacerbated by the other losses of old age. Ecclesiastes 12:1 speaks of the experiences of physical loss as **troubling days** and **years** when people say such things as **I do not enjoy them**.

All in all, there is a gloomy outlook that pervades most discussions of old age. But is that all? Are there no compensations? Is the Christian believer to look at aging as the unbeliever does? The answer to these questions is both yes and no. Clearly, the believer is not to close his eyes to suffering and pain. He is not to minimize or rejoice over the effects of the curse on mankind. He is not a Christian Scientist who denies the reality of sin, sickness or death. He recognizes, with Paul and all of the biblical writers, that the body has been humbled so severely by the curse that man who was to rule the earth is now buried in it. He is realistic. But, as we shall see later on, in Christ, he is able to triumph over these factors. But that is for later. For now, let's pursue the idea that, fundamentally, aging is a process of loss. Let's consider some other losses age may bring.

---

[1] This, apart from Christ, also involves for all the loss of access to the tree of life.

Age frequently leads to the loss of strength[1] and health. For many, this is a large issue in old age (even when it is a fear as much as when it is a reality). Paul's use of the term **decay** in II Corinthians 4 graphically sums it up in one word. This is a strong term. We usually think of decay as something that occurs *after* death, but Paul—ever the realist—spells it out for what it is: he declares that the outer person is already **decaying**! There is no disguising of the fact; the Bible puts it like it is. You may not like to think of living with a body that is already in a state of decay, but it is a fact that becomes more and more apparent in old age. Old age is the time when that decay may lead to operations, organ failures, and other medical problems. It emphasizes what youth and middle age largely ignore. But the reality of decay comes thundering over the phone in clear, unmistakable tones whenever the doctor says (to young or old alike), "The tests show that you have inoperable cancer. I would suppose that you have less than a year to live!" That phone call especially is the fear of many elderly Christians.

Loss of health! This loss may occasion frailty, feebleness, clumsiness, loss of muscular power, loss of skills or abilities. It may lead to fatigue and bad decision-making. One may more readily fall and injure himself. He may find that bones crack more easily. And he will discover that healing—when it takes place—comes slowly. There are innumerable aches and pains. These come more frequently, are intrusive, and may keep one awake for hours at night.[2] Diseases seem to have a more severe effect. New complications may arise. The elderly are more likely to be subject to strokes (now called "brain attacks") or heart attacks. Threats of cancer, dementia and Alzheimer's disease, which loom just over the horizon, may plague them. One may become incontinent. And he may be as embarrassed by the odors

---

[1] Cf. Psalm 71:9, where the psalmist speaks of old age as a time when strength fails.

[2] With all of the attendant problems of significant sleep loss.

that accompany this problem as by the inconvenience it causes. The part of the brain that controls sleep may be hit hard by age, and he may find himself sleeping less at night because of insufficient production of melatonin. He may also discover that the body will not tolerate this, and he may be taking more and more cat naps during the day. He may even find himself falling asleep in a chair while reading! Hearing, sight, and taste buds may all be devastated by aging. Speaking of **decay**—think of this: hearing begins to deteriorate at age ten![1] At age 30 a person averages 245 taste buds; at 75 the average is only 88![2] The result? Food may lose its attraction and poor nutrition may result. Clearly the picture is not a pretty one: the body has been humbled by the fall of man and the ensuing curse!

Then, there is the **loss of stamina**. As they say, "Your get up and go may have got up and gone." You simply can't accomplish as much in a day. There may be a weakening of all the body's systems and the entire system usually works less efficiently. Aches and pains, as well as disabilities, may slow you down. Weariness, the temptation to give up (especially if one has abandoned all ministry), the lack of desire to complete projects (or even undertake them in the first place) may come upon one more and more as he ages. He can be heard saying such things as, "I've done my part in the church for the last thirty years; let the young bucks take over." Of course, there is some truth in this, but . . . we'll consider the rest of the sentence later. There is a loss of alertness; one's reaction time may be off. Driving may become dangerous. Sexual desire may wane.

In addition, there is the **loss of companions and friends**. The most serious may be the loss of one's spouse. Proverbs 2:17; and Malachi 2:14 speak of the "companion of one's youth." One might as readily speak of the "loss of the companion of one's old age." According to Genesis 2:18, **companionship** is the funda-

---

[1] *After Forty,* Better Homes and Gardens (Meredith), p. 23.
[2] Ibid.

mental reason for marriage. This is shattered by death. And, pointedly, the greater the companionship prior to death, the greater the loss with death. Death also may mean moving away from friends, relatives, and loved ones. It is very hard to make new friends. The older one grows, the harder it becomes; there just aren't as many your age around. The church should take a firm hand in doing something about this problem (as we shall see later). Relationships are not "built," as many young people seem to think today. They grow, particularly as people do things together. When people are older there is less time for them to grow; there are less people with whom to grow them; there is less that people find in common to do.

The **loss of independence** also is a problem. Even small, minor, maintenance chores (replacing light bulbs on the ceiling, repairing leaks, etc.) are more difficult, and one may feel "foolish" in asking for help (which may not always be on hand either). Freedom and control of one's environment may be slipping away. One may be confined to a wheelchair, transportation to the grocery store may not be immediately available (driving may have to be curtailed or eliminated altogether), and because of hearing loss, there may not be as many fruitful telephone calls as throughout the years before. One becomes a burden to family or others, and he may be seriously troubled by this fact. Indeed, he may also become a financial burden.

The **loss of a job** may be devastating. Bear Bryant said that when he stopped coaching he would die—and he did! Man was made to work; the loss of that which one has learned to do may be hard to take. Change may come hard; so one may end up doing little or nothing but watching TV. He now has time on his hands. Productivity, the retirement issue, and related matters are of great importance, and I shall consider them later.

The **loss of finances** may cripple one's activities. Usually, finances are reduced. There is the uncertainty about future events that may reduce them even more. For example, fears of catastrophic illnesses, that could wipe out one's savings, grip many. And, if not catastrophic, chronic illnesses may drain finances just as fast. There may be a loss of one's home. Bills for medications may mount. And if the medications are not generic, their costs can take a walloping bite out of a slim income.

Finally, there is **the loss of life** itself. Death is imminent and certain. One may begin to realize that there is not much of a future for him on this earth. A person may become preoccupied with the thought of death, yet, he may not know how to prepare for it. He may fear for loved ones whom he must leave behind.

All these, and I am sure you can add a number more, are losses with which one must reckon as he grows older. Some of them he brings on himself; others he has nothing to say about. They just come. All of them, in one way or another, at one time or another (if one lives long enough) every person must grapple with. But he must do this at a time when he is less fit physically (and in some cases less fit mentally too) to do so. That is the dilemma of old age.

Adam, why did you do this to us? But, on the other hand, which one of us would have done better? And, yet, through Adam's sin (no credit to him) has come something beyond suffering; God has brought redemption in Christ. But that isn't all. In Jesus Christ man has been lifted to an even higher position than he experienced before the fall. In Christ, humanity has been exalted to the throne of God, at the Father's right hand. This, and other important factors, must be kept in mind as a Christian ages and considers death. For the believer, age means not only loss but also gain—great gain. And that is our major interest and concern in this book.

Chapter Two

Some Preliminary Considerations

Given the problems that age presents, many of which we surveyed in the previous chapter, there is little wonder that the world almost totally disparages it. There used to be a time when old age was looked upon with some respect, but in our country those days have long since departed. An older person, it seems, makes every effort to appear younger than he is. Products are sold and services are offered in the attempt to stem (or at best cover up) the ravages of time on the body. Expressions such as "old coot," "old fogey" and the like, capsulize the attitudes of all too many. We are hearing people say that older people ought to give up their place in life to make room for younger ones. There are moves afoot to restrict medical procedures that are costly or limit them to those who are younger ("others have lived their lives; therefore, they should be willing for the younger to receive such treatment"). From time to time extermination of the aged is ventured. And Dr. "death" Kevorkian, though convicted, gets more and more supporters.

George James said, "Age is the most terrible misfortune that can happen to any man."[1] B. F. Skinner, at age 79, wrote, "It is characteristic of our present culture that, with rare exceptions, little admiration and respect are shown for old people."[2] As I noted above, sayings and names—not too complimentary—

---

[1] *Epigrams*, p. 17.
[2] "Across the Board," *Aging*, (Guilford) 1983, p.117.

abound. "The old goat" (from the saying that "an old goat is not respected for his beard") and "the old coote" (probably a corruption of "old goat") and "the old codger" (who knows where that one came from?) are typical derogatory terms attached to persons who may find it more difficult to function than they did when they were younger.

The world insults older persons because they are an unwelcome burden. But they also are a grim reminder of what lies ahead—something that the young don't want to think about. "Get them out of the way—out of sight where we don't have to look at them!" is the attitude exhibited by many. In this regard, Hebrews 2:15 speaks of those who **by fear of death were subjected to slavery throughout their entire lifetime** (cf. I Corinthians 15:56, 57 which contrasts the Christian's proper relationship to death.).

Even the Bible has a description of declining years that the world would buy, since it speaks of the effects of aging from the perspective of those who live only for what they can get **under the sun**. According to Milton Terry, the writer of Ecclesiastes sets forth "the sensualist's dreary view of old age" as an "evil time."[1] All he sees is corruption, decay, and desperation:

> Verse 2 depicts stormy weather ahead. Trouble, like returning clouds rains on one's parade in profusion;
> Verse 3 speaks of the arms and hands feebly trembling, the legs weakened, the back stooped, teeth disappearing and eyesight failing;
> Verse 4 alludes to the loss of appetite and the problem of sustaining a good night's sleep;
> Verse 5 notes how heights frighten, how one fears situations in daily life he never did before, how the hair turns white, how because of lack of strength a grasshopper is too heavy to lift, how sexual desire wanes and

---

[1] *Ecclesiastes* 12:1-7.

that at the end one goes off to the "long home" of death;
    Verse 6 describes the breakdown of the brain, the rest of the body, the heart and the lungs;
    Verse 7 The final touch is the burial of the body at the separation of the spirit which returns to face God.

In all of this, nothing positive is described, nothing hopeful, nothing victorious. All is gloomy and hopeless. As we saw, it is loss—sad and unspeakable loss. That is how the writer of Ecclesiastes[1] wished to describe old age without Christ. He was writing about the way in which those who approach it without a future hope must inevitably see it. These are people for whom the present life **under the sun** is all that there is. For such persons, truly old age offers nothing more than trouble and misery. Because it culminates in death, as he says, it holds the ultimate threat.

"But you said that the Christian life here need not culminate merely in loss. You even spoke of 'gains,' *great* gains to be exact. What of those? That's what I want to hear about." All in good time. I shall get to them soon. But first, let's explore matters from several other angles as well.

I have referred to the words of the writer of Hebrews concerning **those who, by fear of death, were subjected to slavery throughout their entire lifetime** (Hebrews 2:15). The fear of death for unbelievers lies always in the backs of their minds. Often during times of danger, when loved ones die, in days when all seems to be going wrong, this normally suppressed fear emerges in full dress to frighten and even terrify. Age is the reminder of the fact of death. Moreover, it is seen even as the *herald* of death, proclaiming its imminent presence. How horri-

---

[1] There is some reason to believe with modern scholarship that the word translated "vanity" throughout Ecclesiastes (*hebel*) does not mean vanity but rather lack of permanence. Either way, the message of the book clearly seems to be that all eventually slips from one's hands. Change, flux (as the philosopher Heraclitus put it), is all that seems permanent.

ble it must be for a person to continue all his life with no certainty about the future, wondering whether there is life after death and, if so, what it holds for him. No wonder a person looks askance upon old age. It is not that death comes to the old alone (we all know that many die in their youth and middle age), but most everyone *thinks* that he will live to see old age (whether he is right or not).[1] It is in old age when so many other losses occur that these, in particular, are reminders that the ultimate loss may lie just around the next corner. It becomes ever more difficult, as a result, for unbelievers to keep the underlying fear of which Hebrews speaks under foot. More and more often they find that it keeps popping up. That is why so many of them so feverishly throw themselves into every sort of activity to try to ward it off. These frenzied efforts, however, seldom work. Embarrassed, stubbornly determined not to give in to those who have attempted to evangelize them, grasping at straws, many go to their deaths frightened and soured without hope and without a Savior. Others, against all facts, have so seared their minds and consciences that with a foolhardy brashness they plunge into death cursing life and God. In all cases, however, as Hebrews says, every unbeliever has to deal with this fear. He is its **slave**. Like a cruel master bent on getting more than his due, it lies behind every decision and determines much of what he does from day to day. Try as he may, he cannot escape it. Consciously or unconsciously, in clear or unrecognized responses, he will react to death throughout his life. And this is most apparent in his declining days.

Jesus came to deal with this stern taskmaster. Hebrews says that He came **that He might destroy the one who has the power of death, that is, the devil, and deliver those who, by fear of death were subjected to slavery throughout their entire lifetime** (vv. 14, 15). Having Jesus as one's Savior makes

---

[1] Cf. Psalm 49:11. Jerome wrote, "No man is so old but thinks he may yet live another year."

all the difference in old age. There is no longer any **sting** in death (I Corinthians 15:54-57) because Jesus has felt the penalty for the broken law of God. Consequently, death means **to be with Christ which is far better** (Philippians 1:23); this makes an enormous difference in how he lives out his remaining years. One can face death in old age knowing that there is not only a future, but that it will be a wonderful one free from sin and all of its consequences. For the believer, death is a release from the ailments of old age and from the miseries brought about by the curse. Death is the death of death; it can never hurt the believer again (Revelation 21:4). Most of all, it is to be with Christ. That perspective, with all its consequent benefits, must be uppermost in the mind and speech of the counselor who deals with older folks. One of his main tasks is to remind them of the marvelous promises of God to His children.

Not all Christians act as Christians ought (this is true especially of many who need counsel). That is why Paul, in discussing the resurrection of the dead (which some were inclined to doubt), found it necessary to remind them that their **labor was not in vain in the Lord** (I Corinthians 15:58). They had been laying up treasures in heaven where they were protected by God and where nothing could destroy or corrupt them. It was also necessary for him to point out that the stinger had been removed from that dreaded scorpion, death. In the death of Christ, by which He paid the price for the sins of His people, death plunged his stinger into His heart and it came loose. The stinger of death is removed. Death, for the believer, then, should hold no horrors. The devil's **power** to terrify has been removed, as Hebrews says.

Yet, many Christians, because of its finality, because of their **little faith**, and because they may have been poorly instructed, find that the fear of death still does grip them. How is the counselor to help them in old age to dispel this fear? With the facts.[1]

---

[1] Cf. I Thessalonians 4:13ff. where Paul dispels grief by facts that replace ignorance. The work of Christ and the promises of God are heart-warming.

It might be useful for every counselor to print out a list of those promises of God that deal with death to hand to counselees who themselves might have a difficult time searching them out. As an exercise to help you as a counselor familiarize yourself with them, I suggest that you get out your concordance (or computer program) and make a list of all the verses that pertain to the life of the believer after death. From this list select those that seem most clear and most telling and develop your handout to use in counseling older persons.

At some point or other I would make it a regular counseling practice to discuss the prospect of death with older counselees. Whether they admit it or not, the matter has increasingly been on their minds. If they dared to mention it to others, chances are that their comments or questions were deflected by them. All too few persons are willing to speak of death. They do not like to be reminded of the reality and nearness of this grave specter. So, among all the other matters that you will address in counseling the aged, be sure that you give them ample opportunity to discuss the facts of death. This topic may easily be approached through other issues that he raises. For instance, an older person may wish to discuss matters pertaining to the distribution of property or funds. As you deal with such issues you will have more than enough occasions to venture naturally into a discussion of his pending demise. At times when no "natural" transition appears to present itself, there are still ways to broach the subject. When you are looking for them you will find them. When all else fails, there is always the forthright, "blunt" approach. At some point—usually at a time when some other matter has been resolved—you may wish to say something like this: "Now, John, I have discovered that many older people such as you like to talk about death, but can find very few other people who care to talk with them. I'd be glad to. Are you interested?"

Incidentally, if you are reading this book and are unsure of your eternal future after death, you need to get the matter settled right now. Death is certain, one of the most certain events in life, but its manner and its time are uncertain.[1] If you have never done so, trust Christ as Savior. Acknowledge your sin against a holy God, recognize that you deserve eternal punishment for it and believe that Christ died on the cross in your place taking the punishment you deserved. To assure you that God accepted Christ's death as the penalty for His people's sins, God raised Him from the dead. Will you believe today?

In counseling, Christian, as you deal with death and eternity, you will sometimes uncover the fact that a counselee is not certain of his salvation. This is a very important issue for you to pursue. Indeed, in counseling older folks (though not exclusively with them) you will want to make sure that your counselee has assurance. If he does not, that lack of assurance may stem from one of two things. Either he is not a Christian after all (even though he represented himself to be one when he entered counseling), or he may have accepted teaching that has led to his uncertainty. You will want to probe to discover what is behind this uncertainty.

Assure counselees that it is normal for a believer to know that he is such. A child of God ought to be as certain about who his Father is as an earthly one is.[2] There is every reason, biblically, for the believer to have assurance. It is totally unbiblical to teach, as some do, that it is only the 99th percentile of believers who are entitled to assurance. Biblically, there are no first and second class believers. There are those who think that you can be saved and then lost again. This too is unbiblical and, of course, very unsettling. How can one ever believe that he will be saved if his salvation ultimately depends on keeping himself saved?

---

[1] To us death is uncertain. All is certain to God, of course.

[2] Of course, today, many illegitimate children have no such knowledge. I am speaking about the way that things ideally should be.

There are those who think it pious to doubt. But all such persons should be referred to James' discussion on doubt in his letter.[1] James looks at doubt as sin! No matter how you squeeze it, the Bible teaches that the normal state of the Christian is one who knows he is a child of God, who prays "Our Father Who is in the heavens," and who looks forward to eternity with joyous expectation. He knows that he is still a sinner, and he regrets, confesses and repents of his sin; even in despair and sorrow he clings to the fact that he is saved not by his own merits, but exclusively by the merits of Jesus Christ. He has assurance. It is abnormal for a Christian not to know he is one. You ought to use that knowledge to fortify all those who have reason to believe that they are saved. If unconfessed and unforsaken sin in their lives is clouding out assurance, then help them come to repentance. But make it clear all along that the perseverance of the saints not only means that one hangs in there to the end, but also that he does so because he believes that God has not left him or forsaken him. David, in his most wretched and gloomy days of sin and guilt, is still able to ask God to **restore the joy of** his **salvation** (not to re-save him!). At the end of the day assurance depends not on us but on the utterly reliable work of Jesus Christ on the cross.

In the sunset of life, chills of fear about death should not run up the spines of believers. Rather, they should be warmed from basking in the promises of God which, as you gather them for use in counseling, should warm your inner man as well. So you will want to keep in mind at all times the important issues that have to do with death as you discuss those that have to do with the closing days of life.

---

[1] See my commentary on James and my book *A Thirst for Wholeness* which is a practical study of the book of James.

Chapter Three

A Different View of Aging

Thankfully, Christians may have a very different view of aging. It is one that you personally may hold, and that, as a Christian counselor, you can teach to your counselees. It is the view that God sets forth in the Scriptures of the Old and New Testaments which I have already alluded to in passages from Genesis, Philippians and II Corinthians.

While there is in Scripture a clear recognition of the fall, and the misery it would bring (especially for those approaching the end of their lives), nevertheless, there is also a joyous note of triumph that is the hope of obedient Christian saints. The tragedy of aging is offset by the triumph of growingly becoming what God wants one to be. This factor—that I called "gain" over and against loss—is neither Christian Science-like denial nor a Robert Browning-like sentimentality ("grow old along with me . . . the best is yet to be." Obviously, for many, that is not true.). Indeed, the lightness with which Robert Schuller and Norman Vincent Peale approach pain and suffering is in no way akin to the positive things that the Bible teaches. While there is victory in aging, it does not come easily.

"What, then, is the biblical position?" It is a *realistic* attitude, one that makes all the difference. While fully acknowledging the hard things connected with aging this attitude brings to the equation a stronger, more potent counterpart to the negatives of aging. In the truths of the Scriptures we find the promises and power of God for now and for the future. There is hope, great hope, for now and forever!

The world knows nothing about such promises and power so it has nothing substantive to offer the aging. For instance, Robert Butler, Director of the National Institute on Aging wrote, "Old age is the only period of life with no future."[1] With such thinking, no wonder he advised counselors to help old people *not* to think ahead. Can you believe that? Contrary to his advice, Christian counselors know that a large part of a believer's living cheerfully now is the ability to look ahead to a perfect future of happiness and bliss in which sin and all its effects will be washed away. As Peter put it, Christians look for a **new heavens and a new earth in which righteousness is at home**. In contrast to the atheistic view just mentioned, the Christian counselor considers it his distinct privilege to help counselees look ahead to the *greatest* period in their lives. They need to know that **to die is gain** and that it is **to be with Christ, which is far better** (Philippians 1:21, 23).

Anticipation is plainly one of the happiest things that one experiences. If you are going to take a trip, the anticipation is often greater than you find the reality when you actually arrive. From childhood on, people have enjoyed looking forward to happenings. When they turn out to be less than anticipated, it is disappointing. But here, based on the unalterable promises of God, are expectations of a future that will turn out even better than expected! And because the world knows nothing of that future (indeed, it has only a gloomy prospect ahead), it advises counselors to steer the thinking of the aged away from the future.

To be present or past oriented rather than future oriented is to be in a sad situation. The past can not be relived. It is gone, finished. And while it can bring pleasant memories into the present, it can do little to buoy up those who have forever lost that which they remember. Indeed it may present such a contrast with the present that all of the ills and inabilities one is suffering are only

---

[1] *Aging,* Third Edition, Dushkin: Sluice Dock, (1983), p. 19.

exacerbated. And the present is nothing to rave about if that is all one has to turn to in times of distress. The **present evil world** has little or nothing to offer to satisfy the one who is suffering the losses of aging. Because of the insufficiencies of stressing the past and the present, counselors must hold out the future. To remove the one thing left to look forward to is almost criminal. The Christian counselor therefore tells his counselee not to seek solace in past memories and in the world's present offerings; instead he should look forward to what God has laid up for him in the future. It is in precisely what the world seeks to avoid that the Christian exults. Old age, for the believer, is the one period in life when he knows he is soon approaching a certain, joyous future. Counselors must not heed what those with no future advise. The future is a strong weapon in fighting the ravages of aging. Help your counselee to enjoy anticipating it. People are able to endure much when they know that just over the horizon lies something worth looking forward to (cf. I Corinthians 10:13).

"Wait a minute. You were going to tell me how it is good to age *here and now*, not merely to look forward to something after death. I believe in pie in the sky when you die, bye and bye. But I want to know how I can start slicing now!"

OK. OK. Be patient. We'll get there in time. But remember what I have already said: to know about the glorious future of the sons of God is crucial to enjoying old age and the aging process *now*. The future, because it is dependent on nothing less than the absolute certainty found in God's promises, may be enjoyed, in anticipation, as surely as if it were present. The future does affect the present. But now, we shall turn to some other helps that God has provided for those who reach old age.

Let's begin by learning just a bit about what He has to say concerning aging. God's attitude toward the issue should have much to do with how your counselee views it. How he views it will have much to do with how he lives through it.

The Bible makes it clear that God respects age. In Scripture, old age is *desired* and considered a *reward* for faithfulness. In Genesis 15:15 old age is spoken of positively, and it is considered a reward to die **in peace** at **a ripe old age**.[1] In Psalm 91:16 old age is said to **satisfy** and in I Samuel 2:32 it is described as a blessing not to be missed. The fifth commandment (Exodus 20:12) sets forth **long** life **on the land** as a reward children receive for honoring their fathers and mothers. And in Isaiah 65:20 and Zechariah 8:4, old persons' living out of their days and surviving into a good age is considered a fine thing. Clearly the biblical data support the idea that old age is a blessing to be desired. That is not all, however.

Gray and white hair are honored (especially on the head of the righteous. On this matter study Proverbs 16:31 and 20:29). But note especially that God the Father is called **venerable** (Daniel 7:9, Berkeley) and is represented as the **Ancient of Days** Whose hair is said to be white like **wool** (v. 13). God could hardly be described as **Ancient** if, in any way, such a description were a derogatory concept. Clearly the opposite is true. Add to that the description of the risen, glorified Christ found in Revelation 1:14, One Whose hair is **like wool** and white as **snow**, and there can be no doubt that age is venerated in the Bible.

Finally, note that God is *concerned* about the aged: Isaiah 46:4 makes it clear that God will not abandon the aged, but as He has helped them throughout their lives, He will continue to do so as they grow old. That passage, in and of itself, ought to be quite reassuring to those who wonder where God is in their time of loss. Tell them He is just where He always has been. The problem to pursue is where a *counselee* may be in relationship to *Him*. The real issue is about who has left whom.

It is important to note that *nowhere* in all of the Bible is age looked down upon as undesirable (except in Ecclesiastes where

---

[1] See especially the Berkeley Version.

the world's view is set forth); *everywhere* it is considered (even extolled as) a decided blessing. How can that be when, admittedly, there is so much loss?

You must understand the biblical viewpoint, so that you may be able to help counselees also to do so. Psalm 71 is an aged person's Psalm. It is as follows:

1 **In You, O LORD, I have taken refuge;**
   Let me never be ashamed.
2 **In Your righteousness deliver me and rescue me;**
   Incline Your ear to me and save me.
3 **Be to me a rock of habitation to which I may**
      continually come;
   You have given commandment to save me,
   For You are my rock and my fortress.
4 **Rescue me, O my God, out of the hand of the wicked,**
   Out of the grasp of the wrongdoer and ruthless man,
5 **For You are my hope;**
   O Lord GOD, *You are* my confidence from my youth.
6 **By You I have been sustained from *my* birth;**
   You are He who took me from my mother's womb;
   My praise is continually of You.

7 **I have become a marvel to many,**
   For You are my strong refuge.
8 **My mouth is filled with Your praise**
   And with Your glory all day long.
9 **Do not cast me off in the time of old age;**
   Do not forsake me when my strength fails.
10 **For my enemies have spoken against me;**
   And those who watch for my life have consulted
      together,
11 **Saying, "God has forsaken him;**
   Pursue and seize him, for there is no one to deliver."

12 **O God, do not be far from me;**
   O my God, hasten to my help!

13 Let those who are adversaries of my soul be ashamed
     and consumed;
   Let them be covered with reproach and dishonor, who
     seek to injure me.
14 But as for me, I will hope continually,
   And will praise You yet more and more.
15 My mouth shall tell of Your righteousness
   And of Your salvation all day long;
   For I do not know the sum *of them*.
16 I will come with the mighty deeds of the Lord GOD;
   I will make mention of Your righteousness, Yours alone.

17 O God, You have taught me from my youth,
   And I still declare Your wondrous deeds.
18 And even when *I am* old and gray, O God, do not
     forsake me,
   Until I declare Your strength to *this* generation,
   Your power to all who are to come.
19 For Your righteousness, O God, *reaches* to the heavens,
   You who have done great things;
   O God, who is like You?
20 You who have shown me many troubles and distresses
   Will revive me again,
   And will bring me up again from the depths of the
     earth.
21 May You increase my greatness
   And turn *to* comfort me.

22 I will also praise You with a harp,
   Even Your truth, O my God;
   To You I will sing praises with the lyre,
   O Holy One of Israel.
23 My lips will shout for joy when I sing praises to You;
   And my soul, which You have redeemed.
24 My tongue also will utter Your righteousness all day
     long;
   For they are ashamed, for they are humiliated who seek
     my hurt.

Let's take a look at some of the things that the psalmist says about age:

1. In times of trouble, doubt and difficulty the aged person has much to recall as he looks back over God's many mercies to him. When he does so, he cannot fail to recognize God's faithfulness (cf. vv. 6, 17, 19, 20). Here is where the past becomes operative in the present. It is not the past *per se* that is useful to the believer, but remembering the past mercies of God. By recalling them he is able to understand that the God Who has always been faithful to him will certainly continue to be such in days ahead. The past, thus viewed, brings reassurance. Younger persons rarely have so much evidence of this sort to which to turn. An older Christian has much.

2. Older persons who have lived with the Lord over a long period of life, learning about their own deficiencies and their need to turn to God as their Helper, are in a position to realize their present need of Him more than others. Moreover, nothing is said about the fading or decline of God's grace.[1] Aged people may still grow by God's grace (vv. 17, 18).

3. The elderly may continue to be a witness declaring God's goodness to others (vv. 14, 15, 17, 18). There is so much more to tell in old age, and so much more time to do so (cf. v. 15[b]).

Other Psalms speak of the blessings of old age. For instance, Psalm 92:12-14 reads:

12 **The righteous man will flourish like the palm tree,**
   He will grow like a cedar in Lebanon.
13 **Planted in the house of the LORD,**
   They will flourish in the courts of our God.
14 **They will still yield fruit in old age;**
   They shall be full of sap and very green, ...

An older person may be like a fruit-bearing tree that still produces in old age. There is no need to dry up and fade away in old

---

[1] Cf. Deuteronomy 33:25; II Corinthians 4:16.

age (as many do). There is no need for your counselee to waste
the last years of his life watching TV. He may still have a productive place in God's kingdom if only he will. Here is one of
the great differences between those who are happy in old age
and those who are not. People with time on their hands, who do
nothing in the service of Christ, tend to become ingrown, self-
centered, and sicker than those who busy themselves with productive ministry. That ministry may differ from their ministries
in earlier times, but every older believer who is still conscious
may serve in *some* capacity. Part of the excitement of doing so is
finding new and suitable ministries for one's remaining capabilities.[1] Praising God to others and finding something worthwhile
to do for God is the way to stay fresh and green in old age.[2]
When people fail to, they dry up. Old age ought to produce much
praise as well. "But," says one counselee, "I don't know how to
praise God very well." Your answer? "What better time to learn
than now in old age?" Old Augustine said, "I cannot think that it
is at any time of life too late to learn."[3]

Praise isn't always easy—especially when one has aches and
pains. But it is always possible. It must be *practiced*. That is
what the Septuagint version of Psalm 71:24 says, **My tongue
shall practice speaking . . . .** The Greek word used is *meletesei
(to work at in practice).*

People are not to be let off the hook because of age. They
ought to go on learning just as anyone else. In fact, older Christians, because of experience in doing so, ought to be able to learn
more quickly. If they have been learning God's ways from God's
Word all along throughout life, they should find learning to

---

[1] According to Ephesians 4:11ff., all believers are to minister to one another.
Any Christian who is not involved in doing so is not only disobedient, but will
inevitably be unhappy.

[2] Cf. v.14. One is to be **full of sap**, not turn into one!

[3] *Letter* 62. This also would hold true of learning some new skills by which
to serve God.

adapt to new situations according to new truth easier than those who are just beginning. Of course one's ways throughout earlier years will have some bearing on such matters. If a counselee has cultivated a learning attitude and has developed ways to study and apply the Bible, he will go on doing so. If he hasn't, then he must begin. Undoubtedly this will involve effort on his part since there will be much to learn. Yet, he is obligated to do so, and—by God's grace—can. As a matter of fact, there is no age limitation on the promise of Psalm 73:24: **With Your counsel You will guide me**. As Psalm 1 makes clear, that counsel is found in the Bible. And, as he learns and lives according to the Bible, **afterward** God will **receive** him **into glory**. Don't let Psalm 119:100 (**I understand more than the aged**) be true of your counselees. The presupposition behind this verse is that the **aged** are *expected* to know and understand more. That fact is what gives it its point. So in every way make it clear to your counselees that they are to continue learning until the end. And that learning is to be turned into life and praise as well. God does not intend to can and refrigerate those who are up in years. He wants them to be growing green and full of sap!

Psalm 71:14 puts it this way: **But as for me, I will hope continually, and will praise You yet more and more**. The thrust of this verse is that as one grows older his ability and desire to praise God should increase—not decrease! The Christian should gain finishing power at the end of the race. He should run harder (not necessarily physically) rather than slow down in old age. Not only will he have more time to devote to some sort of ministry, but also he should be more adept and efficient, allowing himself by these traits to make up for physical impediments that may otherwise slow him down. It is important for younger people to see the old runner still on the track.

Those who choose in old age to drift do so by choice. There is no recommendation to drift in the Bible. One ought to be able to justify biblically all his choices and activities—or they should be discontinued. Among older Christians you will discover that there is much drift (purposeless action and inaction). Christians may fall into habits that characterize unbelievers who have no reason for living. Always the choice is between drift and drive. While one's physical drive may wane, his spiritual drive within ought not (cf. II Corinthians 4:16[1]). Christians should grow old dynamically, not statically. If your counselees lie down and play dead, that's sin. Tell them to get up, run, walk or *crawl (if that's the best they can do),* but at all costs keep moving toward the goal (Philippians 3:14). There is a great deal of difference between growing older and growing old! The world is full of good starters who—in the end—turn out to be great disappointments.

Not only should one minister in other ways, but there is also a coming generation to whom he must continue to make Christ known. Tell counselees, "If you don't like the way your generation is turning out, you can do something to change the generation to come." That is the burden in Psalm 71:18 and Psalm 78:1-8. Tell them, "If you care about your children and grandchildren (as every Christian should), you may not simply quit and say, 'Oh well, I've done what I can in my generation; let the next take care of itself.'" Urge them to tell their descendants what went wrong and how that may be corrected. Tell them to do everything within their power to encourage them to do better than what they did by more faithfully honoring God in their lives. The older generation, whether listened to or not, has an obligation as well as an opportunity to affect the future for the sake of those to come.

---

[1] This is a very important verse to know and have ready to use in counseling the aged.

Chapter Four

Planned Obsolescence?

We have been considering attitudes toward age. We live in a throw-away society. Hospitals no longer sterilize and re-use medical equipment, but throw it away after one use. We are too lazy to wash dishes so we use disposable paper plates. We discard older models of computers whenever new models with new bells and whistles appear (even when older models are working perfectly well for the purposes for which we use them). It is not out of line, then, to expect modern society, driven by the throw-away philosophy, to consider elderly persons objects for the dumpster too.

The recycling campaign is strong evidence for the extent to which we operate on throw-away principles. The idea is to throw away something, then recycle and reuse portions of what is discarded. There are hints that this mentality may be carried over and applied to older persons as well. Will we soon develop warehouses full of spare parts that are still useful from elderly persons ready to be used as transplants? Or will comatose persons be kept alive as "fields" from which to "harvest" these parts? Any number of present and future scenarios may be envisioned, some of which, doubtless, will be implemented. Faced with that sort of future, what are the elderly to do? One thing is certain—so long as it is possible—Christian older people must continue to lead vital lives.[1]

---

[1] It is understandable that not everyone is physically able to carry on vital functions in the Church and the world. But far more are able than do. It is largely to those that this section of the book is addressed.

Is it necessary for older persons to give up? Must they become senile? Is it right for them to look forward to a period where they are considered obsolescent? The answer to these and other related questions may be found in the passage quoted above (Psalm 92). Speaking of the righteous, the psalmist says, **They will still yield fruit in old age; they shall be full of sap and very green** (v. 14). Surely that description doesn't sound like obsolescence. God's attitude, as it normally does, conflicts sharply with that of the world. An older green tree, thriving and producing fruit, is hardly one that you would uproot and replace with a younger one. It seems that God expects the righteous to lead a vital, useful life among his fellow believers no matter what his age—if only he will do so. Too often, it seems, older persons give up because that is what they are "supposed" to do.

Biblical expectations are important. It will be your task, counselor, to see to it that the elderly persons who come (or are brought) for counseling understand that they must not think that their time is virtually over. Many act as if their task is to mark time until death. You will discover that mentality all too often. For a variety of reasons, people like to have it that way when, instead, they could be rendering significant service to the Lord. Moreover, family members and others who care for them also will have to be encouraged to change their minds about this matter so as to line up with the biblical teaching on age.[1] Otherwise their care, growing out of their attitudes toward and beliefs about aging, will go a long way toward fostering and cementing false ideas in elderly Christians. Vital living to the end is the goal.

---

[1] Often, you will be dealing in the first place with other members of the family. Not only must they be disabused of the "giving up" philosophy but also, in connection with their reoriented thinking, they should be encouraged to bring the elderly person to counseling so that you may be able to discuss these matters with him. Talking about him, rather than to him, is one way of fostering ideas of helplessness.

How does one remain vital in his latter years? Two things are important. First, he should stay current. If he loses all interest in what is happening around him, he will soon become outdated.[1] The tendency will be to stop when it becomes harder to stay current. Reading Christian periodicals, books and literature will help. Sometimes this may mean using a magnifying glass—but it is worth it! He should be aware of what is going on in the world and in the church. He should pray regularly about coming events at his church and for missionaries on the field. He should attend church faithfully (not just when he feels like it) and participate in every activity that he is physically able to.

Second, a believer should always be involved in some ministry. I referred earlier to Ephesians 4:12 where all Christians are called to some of ministry. It is possible that he will have to acquire new knowledge and learn new skills to do so in old age. When presented with this prospect, he must not be allowed to say, "Oh that's too much for me to do at this point in my life."[2] Remind him of the tasks handed to Abraham at age 99! If he doesn't know what to do, he should ask his pastor how he might minister at the church. There are any number of tasks that he might assume to relieve others if he is willing to do some of the things that aren't necessarily up-front-and-center. If he is interested in service rather than applause, he will find more to do than he can accomplish.

If, for some reason, the pastor isn't creative enough to find some regular activities in which he may engage, then the older person may be told he has by that very fact been given one. What is it? It is the task of discovering some avenue of ministry himself that he can offer to his church. Usually it is better to keep quiet about this, working behind the scenes, until he is able to demonstrate to himself and to others that the proposed task is

---

[1] Dressing in an outdated fashion also discourages vitality.

[2] A favorite cop-out is "You can't teach old dogs new tricks." Tell him he is not a dog!

one that he can readily and regularly accomplish. He will then be ready to propose the idea to others.

"Why don't you give me some examples?" To do so would defeat my purpose. Indeed, for you to try to dream up examples for each of your counselees would be counterproductive. Part of what he has is *time*—time he ought to redeem. Time is a precious resource that should not be wasted. It is for him to assess his capabilities and to find the task(s) in which to engage. You should make every effort to convince him that God wants him "yielding fruit" by staying "green." His task is to discover how. You can assign this task as homework. This homework itself may get a sedentary counselee moving. Instead of spending hours in front of the boob tube he can take out paper and pencil and start thinking and listing possibilities.[1] That activity itself should shake loose some of the rust that has been accumulating on his brain. You should not do for him what he has the time and ability to do himself, you will only cater to laziness and inactivity by doing it for him.[2] So urge him to take on this important task. Too often, we expect too little from the elderly. When our expectations live up to their capacities, they often surprise us by what they accomplish.

There are some indications that "senility" is at least in part non-physical. As early as 1984, Ruel Howe wrote, "Autopsies fail to show any constant relation between arteriosclerosis and senility."[3] Muriel Oberleder of the Einstein College of Medicine said, "Frankly, I believe people bring senility on themselves."[4]

---

[1] You may have to instruct him in *how* to accomplish the homework assignment.

[2] Obviously, some persons are infirm. Others may be in a coma. Even then, however, they become useful. In God's providence they provide opportunities for others to minister and for some to earn their livelihood. Never consider anyone a throw-away.

[3] Ruel Howe, *How to stay Younger While Growing Older*, Word: 1984, p.149.

[4] Ibid.

Be that as it may, there are clear indications that the right sort of counseling—counseling that takes God's view of aging can make all the difference in whether one becomes obsolescent or not (assuming that those who will may still live vital lives for Christ). Your task will be to motivate them biblically.

There is other helpful counsel that you may give. One way for older persons to stay on top of things is to align themselves in tasks with younger ones. Urge them to do so. Both I John 2:13, 14 and Titus 2:2-8 indicate that there should be a mix of the older and the younger. These verses show how the elderly may combine their assets of wisdom and experience with youthful enthusiasm and strength to produce better results than if either sought to work alone. Perhaps our Senior Citizen classes and our Young Adult classes tend to rip persons of different ages apart. At the very least, if such groups are to be continued, something else ought to be done in a church to bring them together in fruitful ways.[1] In examining the I John and Titus passages you see that the elderly have much to offer by way of teaching and experience in the service of Christ. While the younger may be out on the battlefield, there is a need for those who have been there before, and now have the seasoning it takes to direct the troops from the command headquarters, to work with them. Moreover, grandmothers are mentioned as having usefully taught the faith to their grandchildren (II Timothy 1:5). For the church not to place the elderly in tasks alongside younger persons is a tragedy for all concerned—including the pastor and the congregation as a whole. The practice frequently leads to foolish decisions, division, and chaos.[2]

---

[1] Everyone is so busy these days it is hard to get them to meetings. Less meetings and more ministering projects in which Christians from various ages participate seems to be the answer.

[2] Part of the problem described in II Chronicles 10:6, 8, 13 was the rift between the younger and the elderly counselors which brought down the kingdom.

In P.G. Wodehouse's book, *Author to Author*, the famous humorist writes,

> You say you tend to get tired nowadays. Me, too. After all, we're both heading for seventy. Silver threads among the gold, laddie. Extract from a book I was reading the other day: "Latterly his mind had been going to seed rather. He was getting on toward seventy, you see." Have you ever noticed, by the way, what peculiar ideas writers have as to what constitutes old age? "He was a man not far from fifty, but still erect and able to cross the room under his own steam," they write. Or "Old though the squire was, his forty-six years sat lightly upon him." At sixty-eight I had reached the stage when, picking up a novel and finding that a new character the author had introduced is sixty, I say to myself, "Ah, the young love interest."[1]

When Wodehouse died in 1975 at the age of 94, he left the nearly completed manuscript of a novel in his typewriter. Here was a man motivated by nothing more than writing novels who never became senile. He was at work until the end. He scoffed at the idea he should become senile and defined old age in his own way. How is it that Christians with so much more to live for, dry up and blow away in old age? How is it that counselors allow them to? How is it that they seldom seek out counselors for help? How is it that their loved ones allow them to deteriorate? There are various answers to these questions. Some are valid ones; many, I fear, are not. In each case the situation must be evaluated. In all too many circumstances, I am convinced, a thorough evaluation would uncover sad neglect rather than good answers.

Then, of course, there is the matter of retirement. In many cases we might call it nothing less than *planned obsolescence*. Young people interviewing for their first jobs today have been known to inquire about the retirement policies of the company

---

[1] P.G. Wodehouse, *Author, Author*, Simon and Schuster: 1962. p. 134.

they are considering. They work toward the time when they no longer have to work! That is a sad commentary on our times. God ordained work as a **blessing** (cf. Genesis 1:28). He did not issue the command to work *after*, but *before*, the curse. The curse made work harder; but work itself is something that God gave to man for his benefit and for His glory. Therefore, let me say it up front, *retirement isn't a Christian option.*

It is hard work to retire. In one of his Father Brown novels G.K. Chesterton makes this provocative, but unexplained statement, "What is absent (for instance) in so many Americans [is] the energy to retire."[1]

Someone has described retirement as "a vacation without an end." Those who retire rarely find it so. We have seen how God expects the Christian to continue to be productive until the end. Bear Bryant, the famous football coach, died just a few days after retiring as the winningest coach ever. On a TV news report announcing his death, he was quoted as having said, "When I stop coaching, I'll die." He did. Indeed for him, retirement was planned obsolescence indeed. Life was over. He had finished living.

The phenomenon is common enough to note. People—many who eagerly looked forward to retirement—find, if they do not die soon afterwards, that it isn't what it's cracked up to be. They die *inside*, curl up, and become lifeless, burying themselves in TV or some other nonproductive activity. People are unhappy when they develop a sense of *uselessness.* As we have seen, God expects the Christian to be productive. Productivity, of whatever sort, requires *work.* One may do different work than before, but if he is *forced* to retire (by his company, poor health, etc.), he should retire to new *work* that he is capable of doing.

There are no *direct* biblical statements about retirement (probably because the concept was not abroad until recent

---

[1] "The Secret of Father Brown," in *The Complete Father Brown* (1987). Hammondsworth: Penguin Books, p. 6.

times). God commands neither "Thou shalt die with thy boots on" nor "At the age of 65 thou shalt retire." However, there are clear *indirect* statements that relate to the matter. In light of the command given to Adam, for instance, absolute retirement[1] can only be considered invalid and harmful. Moreover, the first half of the fourth commandment says, **Six days you shall labor and do all your work.** The commandment has no other limits attached. In Ecclesiastes 5:12 we are told that **the sleep of the working man is sweet.**[2] These are indications that full retirement is not an option. God made man for work; he is not happy when he doesn't work. A new four-letter word for many, however, is W-O-R-K.

Involuntary retirement, stemming from a company's policy or from health considerations is not the sort of retirement I have been referring to. All we are talking about in those cases is what turns out to be retirement from remunerative work. That does not mean that one must retire from work itself. Indeed, he may even be able to continue to work in ways that bring in an income. Either way, he should remain productive. There is no command to remain at the same task until death. David and many of the prophets eventually were called to labor as prophets although they started out doing something else (cf. David, Amos). Abraham in old age was called to move from his home and found a nation. While one may change occupations and activities, and/or slow down as the result of aging, he is not to stop altogether. A full day's work for a 25-year-old is usually not the same as a full day's work for one who is a half century older. We are not equating the two in terms of the amount of productivity.

Mr. Paist, after retiring from the Navy where he was the chief procurement officer for the entire East coast, was able to take a

---

[1] By "absolute retirement" I mean not retiring *to* some other work.

[2] Many have trouble sleeping in old age. One of the reasons for this (not the only one) may be the lack of challenging, tiring work that is done during the day.

job at Westminster Theological Seminary in Philadelphia earning very little in comparison to the experience and the capabilities he possessed. For many years he was able to save funds and tighten the ship until it became a far more efficient institution than it ever had been before. He was able to contribute quite a great deal to the work of the Lord in that way. Many who might do the same, unlike him, have failed to follow up on such opportunities. In this way, not only did he contribute to the Lord's work, but he was able to use the experience he had gained in the Navy, thus recouping some of the tax dollars that believers had paid the government.[1]

The "idle rich" at all ages are a problem for counselors. Like those who retire absolutely, they have time on their hands. Maids do all their housework. Servants prepare their meals. Calvin, commenting on I Timothy 5:6, wrote: "A woman is dead when she is useless and does no good; for to what purpose do we live if it be not that our actions may yield some advantage?" He was speaking of the lifestyle that some women in Paul's day were following. Those who have the money in their older days ought to enjoy using it in the Lord's work so as to be productive in that way. Not everything one earns should be left to one's children. But counselors must also be careful not to get involved in telling older persons how to dispose of their money or possessions. They should steer clear of any suspicion that they wish to profit personally.[2]

The most dangerous tendency of all relating to the matter of retirement is the tendency to retire from Christianity! It is a sad thing to meet those who have been active and useful in the past

---

[1] We complain about unfair taxes; often rightly. But God has His ways of seeing that a Christian's taxes are ultimately used for Himself.

[2] The exception here is if you see a counselee being swindled or deciding to spend the Lord's money foolishly. Even then, it would be important to see that an elder or two from the counselee's church is involved in any help given in this regard.

but who now hardly even attend church, even though they are able to. They have stopped thinking, stopped serving, stopped growing. Their principal problem is laziness. They think that their aged condition is a valid excuse for tapering off. Someone has said "You don't *grow* old; when you cease to grow you *are* old!" *That* is what happens to some lazy Christians.

Counselees should grow until they die, at which time they will become fully grown. If they don't grow at all in old age, one can only wonder whether their profession of faith was genuine. In old age the truth about this often bubbles up to the surface. Under the pressure of the losses mentioned previously, it will become clear if one has inwardly loved this world and has not truly been looking forward to being **with Christ**. If his Christianity seems to be but a veneer, and he is becoming cynical, doubts about your counselee's salvation *should* arise. If he doesn't **bear fruit**, not only does he fail to **glorify God** (cf. John 15:8), but there is also a serious question about whether he is a believer at all (since true believers **stay in the vine** and, as a result, bear fruit; John 15:6).

So, because of the added time, the years of living with the Lord, and the opportunities to lend wisdom to youth in the church, there is no doubt that most older counselees may have a productive lifestyle in spite of their infirmities and problems. There is loss, but there is truly an opportunity for gain as well (and I don't refer only to gain in weight!). But central to it all, is a biblical outlook on age—something that sadly has not been taught adequately by the church and, therefore, falls upon you to do as a counselor. This will be all the harder because it will be incumbent upon you to make up for lost time (perhaps years!). The biblical outlook is that believers are to be growing, productive, vital persons to the end. You cheat them if you aim for anything less in counseling!

Chapter Five

The Problem of Illness

Older people are frequently subject to ills. Some have severely debilitating diseases. It is possible, however, that the sicknesses that they suffer from may be intermittent or chronic, genuine or imagined, self-generated or brought on by outside causes. You must work within these parameters. One of your principal tasks is to discover early on which combination of these factors you are dealing with in a counselee. It may not always be possible to determine these matters as precisely as you would like. Some counselees themselves may not know what is going on in their bodies. Doctors are not always certain.[1] But, to the best of your ability, probing from various angles, you should zero in as closely as possible on the relevant facts. Homework assignments may assist you in determining what you need to know. If a person is unable to accomplish what he is assigned, a discussion of the barriers may, itself, help you gather the information. After you have done what you can, you still may be working in the dark or—at best—in the shadows. Sometimes you may have to settle for this.

The studies show that among older people 20% have no chronic disease and about 6% have at least one condition that does not interfere with mobility and the activities of daily living. Because of stereotypes many dismiss older persons as a miserable, sick, feeble, and problem-ridden segment of society. Studies also have shown that this stereotype is not true. Not only do

---

[1] It may often be necessary to obtain permission from a counselee to speak with his physician.

many elderly people lead healthy, fruitful lives, but more and more of them are reaching the upper age limits. For instance, in 1984 there were 12,000 centenarians in this country alone. So while there certainly is plenty of illness in old age, it is not so pervasive, so crippling, and so determining as it once might have been. You should bear these preliminary factors in mind.

Based on these facts, it is altogether possible that a significant number of persons who claim that they are too weak or infirm to attend church, study their Bibles, or serve Christ in any capacity are wrong. They may, instead, be taking advantage of the aches and pains that most elderly people experience to excuse their laziness. There is a certain sector of the population that whines and complains and, at the slightest provocation, finds it utterly "impossible" to carry on in a normal fashion. The Christian church, as any pastor knows, contains its share of members from this group. Every counselor who counsels the elderly will encounter them.

The problem is, of course, when to spur on counselees who purport to be ill to do better or to acquiesce in their assessment of the facts. Pain is a most subjective thing. There are no objective tests that can definitely determine the amount of pain one is experiencing or what his threshold for bearing pain may be. That is why the ability to do assignments may or may not be the best test you can muster. Of course, when one maintains that he cannot accomplish the task, you have no absolute way of determining whether this is true or not. Though there are notable exceptions, many people will cave in to pain and weakness much too easily. Usually, they can do more—sometimes far more—than they claim or think.

One other factor that you might consider is what others who know them (family and friends) say about what they actually do in other areas. For example, a counselee claims that he cannot go to church because of his pain, but you discover that he sits through 21/2 hour long movies at the theater all the time.

Another claims that she cannot use her hands to staple bulletins for the church, but you discover from her relatives that she knits for hours on end. Those are the sorts of data that should help you in confronting and encouraging elderly Christians to carry on their work for the Lord.

There are illnesses that do not debilitate so severely that one is unable to function. In such cases the task, as I have already noted in previous chapters, is to match a person's ministry with his ability. Too often, because they are not able to accomplish some desired task, elderly people give up and do nothing. They may not even think of the fact that there are different tasks in which they may fruitfully engage. From time to time, some may even refuse to do these new tasks because they are "too menial" (beneath one's dignity), are "not interesting" (as the ones I used to do), or "would involve acquiring knowledge and skills that I would never be able to learn at my age" (translation: it would be too much trouble to do so). The first excuse is a matter of pride, the second is a mix of pride, apathy and laziness, the third is a matter of simple laziness. When you are sure that the task could be readily performed by the counselee who is making some such excuse, you may confront him with the true source of his reluctance. Check out the passages on pride and laziness in the back of the *Christian Counselor's New Testament*. These will help you in dealing with flimsy excuses.

A thoroughly biblical understanding of sickness is essential for the Christian counselor. While any discussion of sickness here can be nothing more than cursory, let me at least set forth some anchor points. All sickness stems from the fall. We experience it because of Adam's sin. Some sickness is the result of God's judgment for personal sin. Other sickness is simply a result of the original curse. It is important not to confuse these matters. Because we know that neither Job's illness nor that of the blind man that Jesus healed (John 9) were the result of the individual's sin, we must be very careful about this matter. On

the other hand, I Corinthians 11:30 makes it abundantly clear
that God brought weakness and sickness (and even death) on
some Christians because of their sin at the Lord's table. So in
dealing with sickness first determine (if possible) its cause.

James 5 offers help in this regard. He writes,

> **Is anyone among you sick? Let him call for the elders of
> the church and let them pray over him rubbing him
> with oil in the Name of the Lord, and the believing
> prayer will deliver the one who is sick, and the Lord
> will raise him up. And if he has committed sins, he will
> be forgiven. So confess your sins to one another and
> pray for one another so that you may be healed. The
> petition of a righteous person has very powerful effects**.
> (James 5:14-16)

The **if** in James' section on illness quoted above distinguishes
between the two causes of sickness that I have mentioned. In all
cases where one is seriously ill, it is his obligation to **call for the
elders of the church**. They are not responsible for finding out
about his illness; he is responsible to take the initiative. He is to
call them. Often the church "grapevine" is operative in commu-
nicating gossip, but it breaks down when spreading information
about illness. There is never a time when it is proper for a sick
Christian to complain that no one from the church came if he
failed to let them know of his illness. On the other hand, in all
too few churches do the elders respond to a call by coming as a
group to minister.[1] Such matters ought to be remedied. As a
counselor, you may find yourself involved in improving this situation.

The elders then attempt to determine which of the two causes
is behind the illness. If it is a sickness caused by Adam's sin (not
that of the sick person) James says that they should prayerfully

---

[1] Some congregations do not even have elders, let alone a multiplicity of
them. There are some broad implications for ecclesiology in these verses.

administer medicine[1] (both prayer and medicine are clearly identified in the passage). The practice of prayer is obvious and needs no further explanation. The use of oil does need to be explained since there has been so much confusion and wrong teaching about it.

Roman Catholics turn to this passage to justify extreme unction. But the passage is not referring to administering a sacrament to those who are dying. Rather, it refers to bringing healing to those who are sick.

Likewise, charismatics and others seem to think that James was referring to a ceremonial use of oil. That misinterpretation is largely due to the poor translation in the King James Version that has often been perpetuated in modern versions as well. The word for ceremonial anointing is *chrio.* That is the term from which the title "Christ" ("the anointed one") comes. It is the word used for anointing as in a ceremony to inaugurate one as a prophet, priest or king (Jesus was all three). But that is *not* the word used by James. As the translation from *The Christian Counselor's New Testament* quoted above shows, the true translation is **rubbing**. The word that James chose, *aleipho,* was used by Greek physicians when writing about the application of ointment (oil mixed with herbs) to a sick person.[2] As the most frequently used form of medicine, **oil** came to stand for medicine in general, and the smearing of (rubbing) oil for the application of medicine.

In addition to prayer and medicine, if it is determined that the infirm person has brought the sickness on himself by sinning, the elders should encourage him to **confess** the sin to anyone he

---

[1] Today, in our highly specialized society, they would recommend medical attention by physicians, not administer it themselves.

[2] Oil also was rubbed or smeared on Greek athletes. For references corroborating this view, see my book *A Thirst for Wholeness,* which is a study in the book of James, p. 134.

has wronged.[1] Moreover, James says that when the elders pray *in faith*, God will heal.

As a counselor, and probably one of the elders, you will find it necessary to question the sick person about whether or not his illness is due to sin. That is probably one of the reasons why elders are to be called. They have care over the flock.[2] They will help in probing into such matters. Perhaps the least intrusive method of questioning with reference to sin is reading this passage from James and then commenting on it. If the person on the bed[3] does not himself respond either by confessing that he has sinned or affirming that he has not, it would then be appropriate to put the question to him: "James indicates that some illnesses are caused by sin, some are not. In your eyes, which of these pertains to your sickness?"

Does God promise to heal all illness? There is no reason to think that He will. Paul, who had the gift of healing, left Trophimus at Miletus sick (II Timothy 4:20); Timothy is advised to use a little wine for his stomach's sake and to help him with his frequent infirmities (I Timothy 5:23[4]). So, it is plain that *if God so wills, in any given instance,* this will be the means by which the person is healed. But the promise to heal is not absolute.

In cases where the person who is healed had committed some sin that led God to strike him with sickness, it is important to follow through afterward. That would mean that the person not only experiences repentance that leads to confession and forgiveness from God and all others who have been wronged, but

---

[1] There is no warrant in this passage for the Roman Catholic confessional.

[2] Cf. I Peter 5:1-4.

[3] The passage presupposes that the sick person has become sick enough to be bedridden. This is clear from the use in the original of the words **pray *over* him**; not simply *for* him. There is no reason to call elders when one is well enough to be up and around (unless the disease is fatal).

[4] In conformity to James, Paul (an elder) prescribes medicine for Timothy.

also seeks counseling to help him to alter his lifestyle in the future. The elders' visit may be but the prelude to counseling.

Sickness, you may point out to counselees, is often the opportunity to grow spiritually. Refer the counselee to the passages in Psalm 119 that make this clear. It would be well to read them in this order:

71 **It is good for me that I was afflicted that I might learn Your statutes.**

75 **I know, O Lord, that Your judgments are righteous, and that in faithfulness You have afflicted me.**

67 **Before I was afflicted I went astray, but now I keep Your word.**

That is what physical affliction should do for those who are ill. It should impress upon the believer his need to be stopped in his tracks and to think again about his life in relationship to God's Word. It should help him recognize that the illness was sent for a **good** purpose. Finally, it should help him change his ways in the future to conform to the biblical teaching that he was either neglecting or violating. God never sends sickness to His children for any other than a good purpose.[1]

That some people waste their pain by failing to realize the reason for it is a sad thing. Teach counselees to squeeze the blessing out of the sickness. Teach them to turn to the **Word** in their extremities. Teach them to praise God for His **faithfulness** in sending illness to drive them closer to Himself. In other words, use these verses to help the counselee to grow in his understanding of God's ways and his conformity to them. This is a *principal* effort to be made by counselors. These realignments of thinking and living are more important than relief. Help the counselee to see so.

Much more could be said about sickness and dealing with it in the case of older persons. Some day, however, if God allows

---

[1] That is true even of the judgments in I Corinthians 11, where the welfare and benefit of the entire church was at stake.

and enables me to do so, I hope to write an entire book on the matter of suffering, pain and sickness in which I intend to enlarge on these matters and introduce many others. But for now, it is most important to recognize some of the factors associated with sickness that bear especially on counseling older persons. Having a grasp on these insights and using them in counseling will make you a much more helpful counselor than the one who merely sympathizes and holds hands!

Now, of course, there may come a time when the following anonymous poem may be true:

Father time is telling me every day
The home I live in is wearing away.
The building is old and for the days that remain,
To seek to repair it would be quite in vain.
So, I'm getting ready to move.

All to the good—so long as the writer has the facts correct and is making no excuses!

Chapter Six

Discouragement, Depression and Despair

Frequently, these three moods so often found in elderly people are closely related. When this is true, in each mood a differing degree of "giving up" prevails. The occasions may differ, but the effect is similar. When you counsel older persons in this state of mind, you will notice right away their dejected attitude. When any one of these problems is present, there is probably no other factor more apparent than this sense of dejection that stems in one way or another from their having given up. You want, therefore, to determine which of these three underlying problems is behind the attitude. The following explains how to distinguish between them.

The difference between discouragement and despair is large, but is mainly one of degree; the dynamic at work in both is very much the same. In **discouragement**, one is disappointed that something he desired has not taken place, and/or something he regretted seeing has happened. He is in a decidedly "down" mood, but he has not yet given up. He may have given up hope of ever seeing the desired event occur (the sought after person return, the perplexing matter resolved, the illness successfully treated) but he is still functioning: he has not given up on *life*! He is dejected, but not defeated.

The **depressed** person, however, *has* given up on life. He says, "What's the use? Why try anymore? There is no more hope for me. People would be better without me." The word "can't" dominates his thought and speech. He has ceased functioning in meaningful ways. He no longer does daily chores, and he less and less assumes other responsibilities. He doesn't find pleasure even in avocations that once brought joy. He is gloomy and sullen. He may eventually contemplate suicide.

The person in **despair** is virtually tearing out his hair over something he considers tragic. He not only is hopeless, but is also in desperate straits over the fact. Anger and frantic emotion may be connected to what he does and says. In this agitated state he may be extremely irritable and at times possibly irrational. He may be unpleasant to the extreme.

In each case the person has *given up*. In his heart there is no longer hope of attaining some end that once meant a great deal to him. Because of the losses discussed earlier in the book, older persons are frequently tempted to give up. Many do. This is particularly true of those who have had their wagon hitched to a falling star, those who have failed to achieve attainable goals because of their own irresponsibility, or those who recognize that life, along with everything they hold dear, is quickly slipping away.

The discouragement, depression, and despair that characterizes each of these situations respectively can be devastating. Not only are they a prime cause of the immobility of the elderly, but may also even bring on an early death as the will to live is sapped. The death of a loved one on whom another depended too heavily, for instance, soon may lead to the demise of the survivor. The first two funerals that I conducted were for a husband and wife who both died within a month of one another. The loss was one that the other did not attempt to find a way to replace. The disappointment was too great because his happiness was fixed only on his wife's presence and attention. Such persons need counsel that points them to Jesus Christ as more important than any mere human being.

Furthermore, a person who has fiddled away opportunities, wasting both time and resources, and who now finds himself physically unable to achieve what he might have done earlier, may pine away in a depressed state for the remainder of his life unless you help him deal with his condition by repenting of his sin and engaging in some satisfying new service for Christ.[1] By God's grace, He may help him **make up for the years that the locust has eaten** (Joel 2:25). A reminder that **where sin abounded grace far more abounds** would also be appropriate (Romans 5:20). Of course, as in all cases of depression, you will begin by assigning the task of fulfilling duties and chores left undone.[2]

There are other precipitating factors that may lead to giving up. For instance take the person who has lost his health through a tragic accident and will never again walk, and who fails to compensate by learning to utilize his remaining abilities, is in a state of desperation over the loss. You must help him to calm down, take stock, place his life in Christ's hands, and move ahead on a new track. Confront your counselee with the principles of a Christian philosophy of life found in Matthew 6; they are set forth there in contrast to the pagan philosophy of life and its attainment.[3] Otherwise despair might overwhelm him.

In all of these situations (and others that are similar) the problem, as I said, is that the counselee has given up. Let us address this matter of giving up, throwing in the towel, or quitting—whichever terminology you prefer. The Word of God speaks expressly to the situation.

The three problems described above may all be met successfully by the careful application of the great passage found in II Corinthians 4. Paul had been speaking of the fact that even

---

[1] Antidepressants may lift one's mood partially, but they make life no more bearable since the real problem is ignored as the symptoms alone are quashed by them. Moreover, they also can bring on many side effects.

[2] For details, see *Competent to Counsel* and *The Christian Counselor's Manual.*

[3] For details, see my *Christian Living in the World.*

though he was burdened for them, most of his fellow Israelites according to the flesh had refused to accept the Messiah as their Savior (II Corinthians 3:12-16). This fact weighed heavily on Paul. Even though this refusal was disheartening to Paul who, were it possible, would have taken their place in hell to save them (Romans 9:3), he says, **Because we have this service to perform as the result of mercy, we don't give up** (II Corinthians 4:1). The King James version reads, **we don't faint**. The New American Standard reads, **we do not lose heart**. The Christian Counselor's New Testament, as I quoted it initially, reads, **we don't give up**. The Greek word is *egkakoumen*, which carries the meanings "to give in to pressure, circumstances; to cease doing something or other, stop resisting, to give up." Sometimes the word has additionally the connotation that giving up is cowardly. At any rate, in verse 1, and again in verse 16, this rare verb is used to speak of the fact that Paul didn't stop what he was called by God to do under the pressure of disappointment by the failure of the Israelites to believe and under the pressure of **all sorts of afflictions** (v. 8). He pressed on through disappointment and discouragement. He did not **give up**.

Now, in speaking to counselees, you need to detail those afflictions that he mentions. Read to disheartened counselees the entire lists of afflictions that Paul records in chapters 6 and 11 of this second epistle.[1] Then ask something like this: "Are your troubles and afflictions greater than his?" An honest answer ought to be, "certainly not."

"Well, you see," you might respond, "If God could supply the grace for Paul to bear up and continue his ministry under circumstances far more severe than those you are suffering, surely He can enable you to do so too."

---

[1] You will never meet a counselee who has suffered as greatly as Paul did. The lists are overwhelming. Reading them in their entirety should bowl over counselees who think that their situation is the worst ever.

If your counselee protests, "But you don't understand what I must bear up under; maybe Paul could stand up to this, but I can't. I'm not Paul," refer to I Corinthians 10:13 (see my pamphlet *Christ and Your Problems* for the exposition and application of this verse on such occasions). Also read and explain II Corinthians 4:8 and 9 for counselees, noting that **affliction** comes, but Paul is **not crushed**; he is **perplexed,** but not **given to despair;** he is **persecuted,** but **not deserted**; **struck down,** but **not destroyed.** Clearly, there is a way to withstand such things. Paul followed that way, and so can your counselee. Note that the trials themselves do not necessarily lead to any of the three problems we are considering. Paul says that in each case there is an alternative. One can stand in the face of great afflictions if he handles them God's way. Take the counselee's words that he uses to describe his affliction, then, filling in the blank, in a fashion similar to Paul, say, "You are afflicted by _____, but do not have to give up!"[1]

How was it that Paul could endure? Verse 1 tells us. He persevered out of *gratitude*. He had received his task from God by **mercy.** He didn't deserve what God had done for him. But he was eternally grateful that it happened. So, whether he felt like it or not, through thick and thin, Paul persevered in his God-given ministry. When you can help the counselee to think and act out of gratitude for the mercy of God shown to him, you will be ready to challenge him to hang in there and persevere in Christian service even through great trials and afflictions. No believer is without some service that he can perform for the Lord (see previous discussions of this matter).

While much more might be written about these issues, remember, older persons are not fundamentally different from

---

[1] Indeed, you might even have a piece of paper on which these words are printed out. Ask him to write out his affliction in the blank space and then take it with him as a reminder. If you do this, it would be salutary also to print out on the same sheet I Corinthians 10:13 and II Corinthians 4.

younger ones. Essentially, their problems are identical. Problems may take on different hues and shapes in old age, and they may carry with them greater temptations that society is all too willing to acknowledge as valid excuses for their giving up. But the temptations, at bottom, are not really all that different. It is not necessarily true, either, that in old age one is less capable of handling difficulties. If anything, a Christian who has been doing so for many years previously will find it increasingly easy to understand how to do so and will easily be able to plan biblical strategies for doing so. If he has not been handling problems well throughout the years approaching old age, however, he may have difficulty. That is why you will want to know something about his current patterns of problem solving.[1] If you discover that he has not been handling life well, as the case often may be, you must encourage him to alter his lifestyle. That will require, in many instances, persuasion and instruction from the Scriptures.

---

[1] Often you may be able to discover these through his responses to homework assignments dealing with specific items.

Chapter Seven

Loneliness

It's true that the elderly are not the only lonely people in this world; but as a group, they perhaps face the prospect of loneliness more than most others. For the most part, however, the essential problem of loneliness is the same at every age. God made man a social creature. The fall occasioned all the problems we now face, including the problem of loneliness. When God said that it was **not good for man to be alone** (Genesis 2:18), He uttered what we should recognize to be a profound truth about human beings: for things to go well, they need others. God's solution to the potential problem was marriage. To a large extent marriage, properly conducted, meets the human need for companionship. In fact marriage, fundamentally, is a covenant of *companionship.*[1] *Companionship is the antidote to loneliness.*[2]

But in a world of sin, marriages go sour. As sad as it is to say, people who live under the same roof may provide little or no companionship for one another. In other cases, marriages break up. And death eventually brings to an end even the most companionable marriage. And in some cases, a person may seek a marriage partner for years without ever finding him. In other words, various problems may interfere with the solution to loneliness that marriage was designed to be. In such cases, the problem of loneliness must be dealt with differently.

---

[1] For details, see my *Marriage, Divorce and Remarriage in the Bible.*

[2] Cf. Proverbs 2:17; Malachi 2:14 where the concept of marriage as a covenant and as providing companionship is clearly set forth.

Any, or all of these problems may be carried into old age. In particular, every marriage will eventually be dissolved by death, if not before. Every married person, therefore, has the prospect of being alone staring him in the face. Since, on the whole, women live longer than men, most wives should be prepared to reckon with this eventuality. Aloneness is not loneliness. The latter is one wrong way of handling aloneness.

In spite of this built in desire for companionship, there are multitudes of older people who spend the lion's share of their remaining days on this earth with no significant companionship. In nursing homes you will find sad and lonely people who sit alone staring out of the window or watching the television most of the day. At "Senior Citizen" functions people pretend to be having a jolly old time. These are just a few examples of the places where you can find many elderly people suffering from the deep loneliness that pervades their lives.

What can be done about it? Counselors, busily carrying on their responsibilities, may not recognize the problem. They may unintentionally ignore it. They make significant contacts all the time (sometimes they wish they could reduce the number). Their friends have not died off one by one until there are virtually none left. They are raising children and busy at work. Often, their problem is to get some time by themselves! So the first thing that counselors must do to meet the problem of loneliness in the elderly is to wake up to it. If you have not given much thought to the issue, it is time that you did. Since God said that it is **not good to be alone**, you must take the problem to heart.

Having gained some understanding of and concern about the matter, what course may a counselor take to remedy it? Well certainly there are many ways to go, some of which are specific to the individual's situation, the environment and the connections that the counselor has. He personally cannot become the companion of every older person he counsels (though, as every believer should, he may participate in lending companionship on some level to some); so it will be necessary for him to find ways to enlist others. Some of this, of course, may be done through elderly counselees themselves. At other times he will have to make contacts for them.

But his help will not always be accepted. There are some counselees who become their own worst enemies. They elect to remain alone. Because of pride they will not take the initiative to enrich old relationships or make new ones. "Let them come to me if they want to be friends," may be one's attitude. Another attitude, resulting in every bit as bad a result, might be something like this, "I don't want people to see me this way, all crippled up with arthritis." Whatever the circumstances, there is a certain number of persons who avoid social contact. They may complain that no one cares about them, but they do everything they can to discourage genuine companionship.

Some older persons develop an attitude problem that drives others away. Those who have tried to befriend them soon come away vowing never to make the attempt again. All they have heard when they were together was gripes, complaints and grumbling. Some are even nasty. They seem to think that their age entitles them to say or do whatever they wish. Few persons want to develop a close relationship with disagreeable malcontents. If time they do spend time with others, some waste it talking about their ailments and illnesses. They can think of little else to discuss because they have lost any vital interest in anybody or anything else other than themselves. Ingrown people are likely to have ingrown relationships—with themselves!

A counselor who is dealing with the problem of loneliness may discover that his counselee is driving others away by his attitudes. He will, therefore, attempt to address the problem not only by mentioning it as a possibility, but also by pointing the way to becoming a more vital Christian that others will want to be their friend. That is one very important solution to the problem. I have mentioned the need for older persons to keep current and to develop interests outside of themselves, particularly in the work of the Lord.

If the older person is involved in a ministry for the Lord, this will automatically bring him into contact with other Christians with whom relationships may develop. I have heard young people talk about "developing a relationship," as if it were something you could do in five easy steps. That is not how significant relationships develop. A relationship is a by-product that grows most often when people do things together. It is not something that you can set out to develop any more than you can set out to attain happiness. These things seem rather to *happen* on their own under certain conditions, especially as persons function together in some activity over a period of time. As a counselor, you should place your emphasis on what counters loneliness. Working together is perhaps the most significant factor. That is why married men and women working together in an office or assembly plant must always be on the alert, watching out lest the wrong kind of relationships develop. Even preachers and secretaries have been known to fall into sinful relationships because they were careless about this matter. But that same dynamic can, as I indicated, also be the good solution to a lonely old person's need for companionship. If he or she spends time working in ministries with other Christians, happily doing the right things together, inevitably a relationship will develop. But the elderly worker should get involved primarily to please God, not to find friends. The latter is a by-product of the former.

Of course, there are the shut-ins to deal with. Even they, however, can develop friendships. It will be more difficult; but if they use the telephone, faxes or internet, they can keep in touch with other Christians who from time to time also may pay them a visit. The church also may help in this regard. It is possible for a church to institute a ministry to elderly shut-ins who live alone. This Older Folks Contact Ministry, serviced by older persons who are mobile, also might foster fellowship and companionship. Regular (perhaps daily) telephone calls to make sure all is well would constitute part of the ministry. On another important front, people might drop in to chat, assess the situation, or find out about needs. The OFCM could provide transportation to the store, the buying of groceries and other goods, and the pick up of items produced or worked on by shut-ins (such as folded bulletins, stapled church papers, knitting for use on the foreign mission field, etc.). The OFCM might become one of the most vital networks in your church. As a counselor (in conjunction with the elders of the church) you might have the opportunity to encourage a likely older counselee to plan, organize and (possibly) direct it. It would be an old folks organization manned and staffed by old folks who through it minister to other old folks in and outside of the church.[1] If special needs arise, this organization could be flexible enough to take on some of them.[2] If your congregation has nothing like this, I urge you to give careful consideration to the general idea. Of course, it needs the oversight of the elders and help from the deacons.

Loneliness can be a large factor in bringing on discouragement. You might want to combine some of the things said in the previous chapter with what has been suggested here. After all, people cannot be divided up into chapters like this book. In many of these chapters we are talking about the problems of the same people we met in previous or succeeding ones. Never get the idea that because one problem is being solved that they all are. Often they form conglomerates in which the various elements must be prized loose so that they can be dealt with separately (as Paul did in dealing with the Corinthian church). But often it is also true that as you begin to get success in one area,

---

[1] Ministering to those outside the church may provide elderly Christians a way to witness.

[2] For instance, some young people need tutoring in math or English. A shut-in might provide the service, but it might take an OFCM member to transport the student to the tutor or vice versa.

that encouragement alone will spark activity on other fronts of the person's life. God created us as whole persons so that everything that happens in one's life affects everything else—for good or for ill. Sometimes encouraging results from attempting one simple thing leads the older person to attempt even greater ones. The bottom line is that the meeting of people through such a church organization produces more interesting and happier persons. Why? One is at work serving the Lord—an essential we have explored already. And to the extent that one's activity throws him into meaningful connection with others, he is at the same time overcoming loneliness.

Granted, the companionship that one finds in intermittent contacts with other Christians cannot begin to replace the fuller companionship that God planned in marriage. Yet, to the extent that it provides solid Christian conversation and activity it will help. God, Who said **I will not leave you orphans**, is the One Who can in His own ways fill in the empty hours. There is nothing that will fully take the place of a properly functioning marriage, but one surely may find a happy, meaningful life if he pursues options like those I have been suggesting (and often that happens only with the help of a counselor).

Many Christians waste their time. The lonely person may profitably spend much of the time praying and studying the Scriptures, that he otherwise might find himself regretting. There are a number of wonderful books to assist him. He has time that should not be "on his hands." He should be taught to be a good steward of his time. Time is valuable and you should counsel him to consider it as such. Rather than becoming sloppy about his habits, he should schedule his time as others do. In that way he will not fritter away his valuable time but may use it in projects that count for the Lord Jesus Christ.

Yet, in spite of all one may do, there will be lonely moments. Even in the happiest marriages, there is loneliness. Perhaps God wants us never to be too satisfied with what we have here so that we will yearn for the heavenly **city which has foundations, whose Builder and Maker is God**. Loneliness, then, can help us to anticipate the future that the Lord Jesus Christ has won for us by His death. That must not be minimized. So help your elderly counselee to thank God even for loneliness and urge him to make the most of it for God's glory!

Chapter Eight

Self-Centeredness

Lying behind much of what I have been saying is a universal problem that, if not corrected, may become greatly intensified by aging. It is the problem of self-centeredness. Every sin, when you boil it down, has at least an element of this in it. If one fails to love God with *all* his heart, it is because he has reserved part of that heart for himself. The same is true with not loving one's neighbor *as himself.* He continues to love himself better than his neighbor. It is no wonder, then, that as a counselor of older persons you will run into those who are so completely bound up in themselves that you wonder whether there is *any* place for God or their neighbor!

I said that aging may intensify the problem. That is because the aloneness mentioned in the last chapter and the aches and pains (not to speak of more serious illnesses), as well as the other losses endured, daily call attention to themselves and tend to direct one's focus on what is happening to one's self. In other words, the squeaky wheel gets the grease. Moreover, since one will soon go to his **long home** (as Ecclesiastes puts it), he may concentrate more on his immediate future than at other times. If he is not involved in some meaningful, fruitful ministry, if he is not socializing with other Christians while doing so, and if he has not learned to live happily with God, who is there to focus on but one's self?

So, the temptation is great. How may a counselor recognize when he is dealing with it? One obvious way is the amount of talk that one engages in concerning himself. If a shut-in has no other regular contacts and fails to keep up with what is going on in the world, his world will shrink to the space within the walls where he lives. You can see this in a hospital patient most clearly. For the bedridden, every wrinkle in the sheets can become mountainous to him. If all that he is living for is self, even a slight delay in delivering the next meal may mean that he will reprimand the orderly unmercifully. All these things may characterize unfaithful Christians as well as unbelievers. Christians are still not entirely sanctified—far from it! They too are subject to a great deal of self-interest and self-centeredness. If one's lifestyle has been centered on self, that fact will be exaggerated in old age.

Then add to that normal[1] mix the fact that an entire generation (with which some of you will have to deal) has grown up under teaching focused on self-love, self-esteem, and self-worth.[2] This unbiblical viewpoint has been accepted and bunged into the Christian church by eclectic believers and propagated by some of its most outstanding personalities. When the people taught in these self-love doctrines grow old, when everything fails to go their way, and when no one considers them #1 any longer, remember what intensified their problem. You may have to let them down hard by informing them that Christ, not they, must be first! Great damage occurs from bringing the world's philosophy into the church. Don't make the same mistake again in your generation with the next pagan fad that comes down the pike.

There are people who have been told that they really are something! They have been led to believe that they are God's gift to the universe. From childhood, they have been driven about in automobiles boasting bumper stickers that say, "My child is terrific!" And they have believed the lie. They have been taught the insidious philosophy of Abraham Maslow that unless others first

---

[1] That is, normal for sinners.

[2] For a full biblical analysis of this movement and its teachings see my book *A Biblical View of Self Love, Self Esteem and Self Worth.*

love them, they are incapable of loving others. This devilish philosophy of life does nothing but first and foremost focus all their attention on themselves. One can imagine what such persons will be like in old age when everything they have tried to live by no longer holds true for them.[1]

At any rate, you will have to deal with people who are self-centered and growing more so every day. This can automatically happen to people when they drift. Unless one recognizes his need to love God and his neighbor and is actively developing a heart for doing so, he will drift into sin. We are all born with a self-centered focus. It takes active thought, commitment and action to grow by grace in the right direction of becoming other-centered. Often the loss of interest in one's faith may accompany the losses of old age. When one is unable to attend church and no longer is involved in what is happening there, and if he doesn't make a determined effort to keep up in spite of being shut-in, he will soon go to seed. This is doubly true of those who are able, but *choose* not to attend the services of the church.

The words of the 90th Psalm need to be emphasized. There the shortness of life is set forth and the need to **number our days that we may apply our hearts to wisdom** (v. 12). That is the answer to self-centeredness and so many of the other problems that we have been encountering. What that means is that we should grasp the fact that we have just so long to live here and that there is much **wisdom** to be gained in that brief period (normally 70-80 years; v. 10). If we fail to acquire wisdom and to live by it (on the crassest level) we enter into eternity with few treasures laid up for ourselves (Matthew 6:19-21[2]). If we do not cultivate a love for God and for others, we are wasting our time here. The psalmist is realistic. He recognizes that we are sinners

---

[1] One can only hope that as the fads change they will be disabused of much of this philosophy before reaching old age.

[2] Note: the less treasures you have in heaven, the less your heart longs to be there (v. 21).

and live under the limitations and many vicissitudes of the curse as we plod our weary way through this brief span of life (v. 9). That is why he exhorts us to **number our days**. He calls on God to help him do so, just as we should every day of our lives. The idea is to number our days so that we may make the most of them. In the New Testament, the corresponding teaching is to **take advantage of the time since the days are evil** (Ephesians 5:16). Applying one's heart to wisdom means learning so as to live it. Wisdom in the Bible is the practical expression in life of the truth of God. It might even be thought of as daily worship, since life *is* worship for the obedient Christian.

I have spoken of the concern for serving God that you should attempt to instill in counselees and given one suggestion in the last chapter about how to reach out to others (love for God and for others Jesus said is the summary of the Old Testament Scriptures). Let me here simply emphasize that this is the supreme effort that you should put forth. Your concern ought to be to point the ingrown counselee away from his self-centeredness toward God and others.

You may have to emphasize to him the amount of talk he engages in that is self-centered. You may need to point out to him that he knows little or nothing of what is happening at his church. You may find it necessary to virtually quiz him in order to learn how bad things are. Say you have a shut-in to whom you are talking during a pastoral visit who seems to be all tangled up in his own interests. You ask, "Have you been getting the church bulletins through the mail regularly?" The response is positive. You then begin to discuss some item in the bulletin (perhaps what went on at DVBS), and your counselee looks puzzled. You then ask, "Didn't you notice that we were having DVBS?" The reply is negative. You now suspect that your shut-in probably considers the church bulletin of little or no significance. It may be time to bring him to repentance and a change of practice for not caring enough even to read the bulletin. You may challenge and encourage him to pray for and inquire about items mentioned in the bulletin.[1] And you may even want to give him the assignment to make one particular area of church activity his major concern. His regular prayer for and interest in it (exhibited by inquiries and by visits from those involved) may be a vital factor in his life as well as in the life of the church. Perhaps the shut-in may keep a prayer diary concerning the activity and those associated with it so as to remind himself of what is happening and to make his prayers meaningful. There are many ways in which he can be involved, if he only will be. He may write letters, send cards, or even make brief telephone calls[2] to those involved in the activity. On the other hand, those involved may call with prayer requests from time to time or may report results. They will be more likely to do so if he shows real interest. If the shut-in's special relationship is understood by all concerned it is more likely that a solid, helpful relationship will develop.

Throughout your contacts with the counselee, self-centeredness must be dealt with above board. It must be called what it is—sin. We are not talking about legitimate concerns for self (hygiene, calling for the elders when ill, etc.) but a first-above-all centeredness that dominates life. Psalm 90 is straightforward about how God's anger with sinners reduces them once again to **dust** (vv. 3, 7). He does not fail to recognize the need to exhort sinners to **number their days and apply themselves to wisdom** (otherwise they might not). You must lovingly be clear about such matters as well. But along with that is the need to give practical suggestions about how one may do positive things that will help preclude self-centeredness in the future. It should never be busy work but always work that is useful to the kingdom of

---

[1] He may keep up on things in more detail by talking to people from the OFCM when they visit.

[2] Too many calls, or calls that are too lengthy, also may signal self-centeredness.

Christ. We have spoken of the need to remain (or become) vital persons in old age. A vital person is never self-centered.

Along with self-focus comes self-pity. That is another sign of major self interest on the part of a counselee. If he is always whining, wondering things such as, "Why did God do this to me? Why now? Why this?", and is not really interested in a biblical response to his questions, you can be relatively sure that the self-centered dynamic is at work. How can you tell whether or not he is interested in biblical answers? Well, after you give him an answer, does he complain less and engage in meaningful conversation growing out of your answers? Or does he simply go on whining as if you had said nothing at all? Observing such things will be a dead giveaway.

You must cultivate attitudes of cheerfulness, thankfulness and excitement in such persons. But these things are not compatible with self-interest and self-pity. Thus the counselee must replace the latter to become a vital person once again.[1]

One other matter should be broached. It has to do with all older persons, but is of special concern to those who are used to expecting others to do things for them. It is the problem of *self-motivation*. In this case self concern is appropriate. In order to not lead a self-centered, dependent life, one must reach the place where he has learned self-motivation. Another word that doesn't quite equate but is closely associated with self-motivation is personal *responsibility*. Too many older persons want to be waited on. Self-centered persons will rely on others to do for them what they can do for themselves. There can be a great deal of manipulation involved. This attitude contrasts sharply with Galatians 5, where among the fruit that is mentioned is **self-control**. Not only does one reign himself in, but also has to have such a grasp on himself (as a result of the Spirit's sanctifying work) that he is able to lead a life that is dependent on no one but God. The

---

[1] If, indeed, he ever was. Sometimes it is in the later years alone that this may happen.

church is there to help, of course. Brothers and sisters are supposed to **bear one another's burdens** (Galatians 6:2), but only in order to enable others to **carry their own loads** (Galatians 6:5). The direction and manner in which one runs should not be turned over to another if it is at all possible for one to assume normal responsibilities for himself. That, then, is your task—to get the older person up and running on his own.[1] It is important that they hold the course, so as to finish the race (II Timothy 4:7). Indeed, the last part of the race may be the most important.

Unless one has totally given up, he will be neither happy nor satisfied with others taking up responsibilities that he ought to carry. One will probably have at least a tinge of guilt, and rarely will others who are being manipulated into such activity do things the way one wants. For true satisfaction, the counselee should be encouraged to take on every task that he is able to shoulder. He will be happier for it, and he will be showing love to others who have enough of their own responsibilities.

Here is the heart of an effective ministry to the elderly. Don't fail to pursue it with vigor.

---

[1] That is, as much as he is able to carry in his present physical condition.

Chapter Nine

Anger, Bitterness and Cynicism

Closely related to much we have discussed is the problem of anger, bitterness, and cynicism. Christians who have never been confronted about their sinful attitudes, and who have developed wrong views of aging and its attendant difficulties, are among those with whom counselors must frequently deal. It is not a pleasant task since the counselor may become the target of their venom.[1] One's complaining, self pity, focus on himself, and other such wrong ways of handling age's difficulties, in time may brew a very nasty stew down in the heart. It is the counselor's duty to expose this, deal with it definitively and help such counselees develop the biblical alternative to their sinful practices. It is not an enviable task; but it must be done.

Since by their attitudes most persons of this sort have driven others off the counselor may be the only person who spends much time with them. That may mean, as I said, that he is the one who will bear the brunt of their anger. While he should not take this to heart—as if he were guilty of causing it in his counselees—he will find it necessary to endure and confront it. Often that confrontation, in which he points out the sin involved, will be the catalyst for the release of even greater bitterness that has been stored up over a long period of time. He will use such pas-

---

[1] A counselee out of desperation may turn on the one who is seeking to help. He cannot enjoy the attitudes that he develops even though he may attempt to justify them. Consider such outbursts as cries for help.

sages as Ephesians 4:29-32 to deal with this matter. When blame is shifted to himself (the counselor) or to others, he will observe that no one else can cause a counselee to act or speak with bitterness and resentment. The counselor will refuse to accept personal responsibility for things that he has not done. Instead, he will place the blame right where it belongs—on the counselee— and call him to repentance.

Persisting in this stance ultimately should bring change, if the counselor doesn't waver and if he holds out a new and better biblical way. If he waffles while under attack, however, he may do more harm than good. If no change occurs even when the counselor does not give up, this should cause him in time to question the counselee about his profession of faith. It might even lead to church discipline. It should not be unheard of to discipline older counselees so long as their mental capacities are still intact. Perhaps, after causing their share of problems in congregations and among family members throughout previous years when they ought to have been disciplined (but weren't), they at last may meet someone who cares enough to apply the principles of Matthew 18 to them before they die.[1] The prospects of this may initially seem horrendous to a counselor whose heart goes out to the elderly (as it should), but when he recognizes discipline as the kindest thing that can be done, his love and sympathy for the counselee will come into line. A physician will not hesitate to operate on an older person if he believes it will enhance the remainder of his days. Why, then, should a pastor or elder who believes in the remedial power of church discipline be reluctant? After all, Christ promises to work through the process (Matthew 18:20).

Bitterness is **anger** stored up rather than dealt with. **Cynicism** is an attitude that says that nothing really matters; every-

---

[1] For help in this matter, see my book *A Handbook of Church Discipline.* Remember, church discipline is a right and privilege that has as a major objective benefit to the one who is disciplined.

thing that others think is important really isn't. It pooh-poohs the motives and concerns of others as worthless. It assumes a superior attitude toward institutions and people that declares them hypocritical and fraudulent. Because of this attitude, anger may develop; and after a time bitterness may result. The older person, caught in this trap, is not a pretty sight.

True, there is much hypocrisy and fraud. True, there is lying and cheating on every hand. True, the wicked often prosper (this is not a new phenomenon—read Psalm 73). But none of these things justifies cynicism. Nothing more than wickedness is to be expected from the world. Romans 8:8 says plainly that those who are in the flesh (unsaved persons) cannot please God. Any Christian who has studied his Bible ought to know that. It should come as no surprise, even to the neophyte believer, that unbelievers lie, steal, cheat, and the like. He has a hard enough time himself refraining from such things!

Well, then, why *not* declare the whole mess worthless? Why *not* become angry over those who have done wrong to you? Why *not*, after experiencing so many instances of the sort over a long lifetime, at length become bitter? The answer to that is found in I Corinthians 15:58:

> **So then, my dear brothers, be firm, immovable, always abounding in the Lord's work, knowing that your labor for the Lord isn't worthless.**

What the Christian does in this life counts because life here is not the end. He is able to lay up eternal treasures in the heavens. So, holding fast to this promise found at the end of Paul's long discussion of the resurrection of the believer, a Christian must declare that he is no cynic because *God* doesn't lie, cheat or steal. *He* is no fraud! If after proper confrontation (in love) and a full discussion of this verse your counselee fails to repent of the cynical and bitter attitudes he has fostered, it is possible to conclude that the counselee may not really be a Christian after all.

There is another possibility, though (never jump to conclusions about a false profession of faith too readily). It could be

that the counselee in question knows little about confronting others, granting them forgiveness upon repentance, and all that is
involved in the process. Churches have been remiss in teaching
about and modeling biblical relationships. I am not about to
launch out into an extended discussion of forgiveness. That can
be obtained in my book *From Forgiven to Forgiving* in which I
deal with the ins and outs of forgiveness as they apply to counseling. If you are vague about the subject, by all means I urge
you to obtain a copy. Counseling cannot be done without a thorough grasp of the subject. There is much wrongheaded, unbiblical nonsense bandied about concerning forgiveness that needs to
be corrected. Much encourages self-centeredness. Perhaps your
counselee has been wrongly informed about the biblical teaching
and is now reaping the bitter fruit of the error. If so, it is about
time to straighten him out. But first you must be sure that you
have things straight yourself.[1]

When there are others with whom the counselee has not been
reconciled, in time that can lead to bitterness. The passage in
Ephesians 4 commands him to **not let the sun go down on his
angry mood.** There are counselees who have let many moons go
down! I have written extensively about this matter elsewhere and
will not repeat here what I have said previously.[2] You must
probe to see if there are people with whom the bitter, resentful
counselee is unreconciled. The chances are that there is at least
one. Don't miss the opportunity to help him become reconciled
with that person (those persons) before death makes it impossible.

The cure for bitterness, I have said, is found in the teaching
of I Corinthians 15:58. But the words of Ephesians 4:23 also
should be in the back of your mind as you endeavor to bring a
counselee to the place where he abandons his cynicism. The

---

[1] Study carefully such verses as Matthew 5:23, 24; 6:12, 14, 15; Luke 17:2-
10.
[2] See especially *Competent to Counsel.*

verse is sandwiched between the two verses that teach the **put off/ put on** dynamic of sanctification. It specifies the motivation for removing sinful patterns and replacing them with righteous ones. There Paul writes about **being renewed in the spirit of your minds.** Actually, there are two words in the Greek New Testament for "renewal." The one found in Romans 12 and in Colossians 3:10 (parallel to Ephesians 4), *ananeoo,* means "to make new again." It is a colorless word that doesn't tell us *how* that renewal takes place. However, the word in Ephesians 4 (*anakainoo*) does. It means "to make young, youthful again." Perhaps the best translation of the word, then, is "rejuvenate."

Think of what the world was like for Adam before the fall. He looked out on a perfect planet. He saw it with righteous eyes. In his heart was the prospect of subduing and occupying it as God had commanded—all to His glory. It must have been a wonderful attitude with which he contemplated the future. Then sin came with all its ugliness and misery. Over the years, an older person has had the opportunity to taste the many bitter fruits of sin. He has become cynical. But coming to know Christ and the truth of I Corinthians 15:58 should change all that. He should understand that what Adam lost he may regain. Not only can he regain it, but by God's grace he can receive even more (all that eternal life holds for him)! He has the prospect of **a new heavens and a new earth in which righteousness is at home** to look forward to (II Peter 3:13). That should **rejuvenate** him in **the spirit**[1] **of his mind.** With that sort of attitude, he may face the trials of old age with enthusiasm and courage. It is your task as a counselor to so paint the picture for him that he not only can see

---

[1] Here **spirit** ought to be translated "attitude." It is a matter of one's mental attitude that is in view. The attitude of cynicism must be replaced with a new, youthful one. Youth looks forward to the future and works with hope and enthusiasm. That is the spirit (attitude) you need to inculcate in the aged person in place of his cynicism. Only by such a spirit can he replace cynicism. How delightful it is to meet an elderly Christian with a youthful spirit!

the prospects in vivid colors and hues, but also will yearn for it with joy. That is the sort of counseling that nouthetic counselors engage in. It is not all just confrontation with accusation; that exists—when it does—only to make room for confrontation about joyful anticipation! We are never to be problem-oriented; only solution-oriented (as God is).

Dr. Kevorkian has received publicity because there are those who wish to promote assisted suicide in old age. The Hemlock Society is perhaps the most vocal group of this ilk. But suicide is self-murder, and all murder is forbidden by God's commandment. Twenty-five per cent of all suicides in the U.S. are by persons over 65 years of age. Suicides are not caused by low self-esteem, as some have erroneously taught, but from the opposite. When a person believes he should receive more from others than he gets, he may become bitter, angry and resentful enough to say, "I'm too important to be treated this way. I'm getting off the world!" It is inextricably intertwined with cynicism. With the growing pressures toward euthanasia (cf. the Netherlands) there will be more and more people who in their cynical, self-centered way take their own lives. Such persons focus only on self. They don't care about what their act will do to those who are left behind. And, most of all, they care little of what God thinks. You must tell the elderly who speak about suicide[1] that no Christian may ever rightly contemplate it. It is sin even to entertain the possibility.

Bitterness, anger, cynicism are all self-destructive. They close one off from others and from all help. So long as this spirit persists, you will not be able to be of much help to counselees.

---

[1] All such statements must be taken seriously. Until the threat is past, someone should be in touch with the one who is speaking about taking his life. Ultimately, however, if a person is bent on suicide, he will find a way—usually in spite of every precaution that is taken. While a counselor should be sad if this happens, he must not berate himself for it. Even if he did all the wrong things, that does not justify self-murder as a response.

You see, in dealing with persons there are always three matters to take into consideration: the **issue** ("Those people have wronged me"), the **attitude** ("I am very angry with them") and the **response** ("I refuse to talk to them any more"). It is useless to deal with the **issue** until the **attitude** is changed. The reversal of the **response** will be of little value without a change of heart. So always deal with the expressed attitude.[1] Repentance takes place within and leads outward to the counselee's dealing with his responses and the issues that have arisen between him and others. Keep that in mind.

---

[1] You can deal only with what you see and hear. God alone has the right to search hearts.

Chapter Ten

False Expectations

I have already mentioned the matter of hope in several places. The Christian has hope and may reap present benefits from it. The word **hope** in the Bible means more than our modern concept. For us, **hope** is an uncertain thing. When we use the word we often mean no more than "hope so." In Scripture, the Christian hope in no "hope so" hope. It is a confident expectation, a joyous anticipation of something that is just as certain as if it had actually occurred. That is because the Christian hope is based on the unfailing promises of God.[1]

Hope is essential as one looks forward to death. The Christian gladly looks forward to meeting his Lord upon dying. Death, as we said, is **far better** because for him it means to be **with Christ**. However, there are false expectations both here and for the future with which counselors must reckon. Let's look at a few.

Take the following sentence, for instance: "When I grow older, things will stay largely the way they have always been." Well, that is certainly a false expectation if there ever was one! Not only will there be changes in one's body as aging occurs, but also the circumstances in which he finds himself cannot remain the same. Friends move, die or desert. Family members do the same. The situation at the church one attends will not remain static. In a few years a once growing, peaceful congregation may become embroiled in a knock down, drag out, pier nine fight when the new pastor comes. Finances, which have been stable,

---

[1] Cf. I Peter 1:3-5.

may now fluctuate because of the loss of one's former livelihood. And on, and on, and on! The only thing that stays permanent in this world is change. Anyone who thinks otherwise
should talk to a number of older persons about the matter. To
deny that there will be no change as one grows older is to deny
reality.

The important thing to do when counseling persons who are
thinking about aging (or who are in its early stages) is to help
them learn how to deal with change biblically. Change is something that believers, of all people, ought to be able to handle best.
We *believe* in change. Change in ourselves ought to be occurring
all of the time. If the Spirit of God is present, there is spiritual
life as well. Life means growth; growth means change. If one
recognizes this and delights in it, he can look forward to old age.
He may anticipate with joy becoming more and more like Christ.
If, indeed, a person experiences no change, and all things remain
as they have been for years, there is something radically wrong
with his Christianity.

A change in circumstances can be an adventure with Christ.
Who wants the status quo? People who fear change or who are
satisfied with what they are and what they have. None of these
stances ought to characterize the believer. He ought not to fear
change, because change is an opportunity to serve God new
ways in different circumstances. Ultimately all change is from
God Who, in His providence, orders all things. Change is not
just something that happens; it is something that happens
because God wants it to happen. Although the believer cannot
always determine how a given set of changes in the circumstances will turn out for good, he can know that this is true
(Romans 8:28, 29). Abraham in his old age packed his bags and
wandered into an unknown land at God's behest. You may have
to do the same. But so long as you know that God is with you, **by
faith** you too may travel in security and anticipation of what
God is about to do in your life.

Furthermore, no believer should be satisfied with things as they are. There should be growth not only in his spiritual life, but also in his ministry for the Lord. Every change in life's circumstances provides a somewhat new and different opportunity, not only to learn to trust God, but also to minister. If one spends his time wringing his hands over change, he will never see it that way. If, on the other hand, he looks forward to those opportunities, he will find more of them than he is able to seize upon. So change, for the Christian, ought to be an adventure with his Lord. That is what counselors need to help counselees see and pursue. Otherwise they will be unable to handle the many changes that are going to come their way.

Let's look at another false expectation. Consider this statement: "At least I can keep all that I have." There is no certainty of this. Indeed, all the odds are against it. Surely as death approaches, the prospect of the loss of all temporal things ought to become apparent. But even as one grows older there will be many inevitable losses. Perhaps the loss of a spouse will be the most pronounced. Then there may be a large house that cannot be cared for; this may require a move to a smaller apartment. That move may also mean that many items must be sold or given away to the children. If one's fingers become all cramped up with arthritis, for which the doctors say there is no remedy, then why not sell or give away the piano? If one's eyesight is failing, and there is no remedy, then the next item to go will be the car keys. And with that goes mobility. And so it goes! No, it is a false expectation that one may hold onto people or things as he grows older. More and more will tend to slip from his grasp.

This loss of people and things once again affords the believer an opportunity. It is an opportunity, prior to death, to experience living with and for the Lord in ways that he never learned before. He may have been all too dependent on other persons and on things. Now that these are melting away one by one, he may learn to depend on the Lord in new and greater ways. As he becomes less and less dependent on anyone or anything here, God provides a situation in which he may learn greater trust in and dependence on Him.

How do you help the grieving Christian do so? He is sad over his losses. He looks on them as a great tragedy. Well, there are a number of things that may be done besides teaching the truths that I have been discussing. You may help him to see that as he sells things he may be able to use the funds to support some project at his church. He now can think happily of how funds from the sale of that grand piano became the means of supporting a group of young people going to Costa Rica to help missionaries. Say out of that, at least two of those young people decide themselves to pursue training for the mission field. His piano was no loss; it was all gain!

Another possibility, by which he may turn loss into gain, is to enter into the joy of giving things that he has treasured over the years to each of his children. He may even decide that on every gift-giving date (Christmas, birthdays, anniversaries, etc.) he will allow a child or his spouse to come and pick from certain designated gifts one or more that he would like to have. This certainly is a more pleasant way to dispose of one's belongings before death than to wait and think of them squabbling and fighting over them when he dies. It is sheer stupidity to think that one may hold onto what he has for the rest of his life—unless, like the rich farmer who built larger barns, this is his last night on earth![1]

Let's look at one more false expectation: "When change comes, and I am forced to make adjustments, I will still have my children to bring me happiness. They can bring joy and meaning into my old age." Tell him, "Whoa! First, what makes you think that they will be around you to do so? They may be required to relocate because of a job change. Moreover, even if they live

---

[1] See Psalm 49:10.

next door, they will not have time to cater to you—especially, if they are trying to support and train a growing family of their own. And, last, but of the greatest importance, *no one—not even children*—can do what you think. If you are going to be happy and satisfied in old age, it will not be because of what others do for you. It will be because you have learned to live a contented life with your Lord. It will be wonderful if your children do love and care for you in old age, and they surely can make the period one of greater joy than if they did not. But they cannot do for you what you must do for yourself. Their best will be like the cherries and ice cream on top of the pie. But you must bake the pie yourself!"

The final false expectation about aging that I would like to mention is one that all too many believe. "Now I can relax and I will no longer find it necessary to assume any more responsibilities." I have addressed this idea to some extent in Chapter Four. But let me say at least this here: the person who avoids as many responsibilities as possible is the person who avoids as much happiness as possible. Everything worthwhile in this life involves taking on responsibility. That which is unencumbered with responsibility is hardly of significance. Think this through and help aging counselees to understand it. If one wants to sell certain pieces of furniture and give the money received to the church to finance some project, as I suggested above, that involves responsibility. He must make many decisions and become actively—responsively—involved, doing things such as advertising the item, talking with people on the phone, and arranging for the transfer of the money to the church. If he simply waits for others to do things for him, he misses the joy of participation in all of this. He becomes passive rather than an alert, aggressive "go getter"!

All of the things in this chapter are but suggestions. We could mention many other false expectations, but these are enough to help you think about the matter when counseling.

Don't fail to address such false statements as those I have mentioned here, work them out for the counselee (as I have attempted to), and help him to think more realistically (which is to say, biblically).

Chapter Eleven

Planning and Scheduling

I have already mentioned scheduling, but it is now time to go into detail. I also mentioned the dangers of drift—simply allowing things to happen instead of taking control of one's time and interests. It is my observation that very few elderly people plan their days with any sort of rigor. The ones who do are probably those who throughout life did so, and are now, so far as is practicable, continuing the practice. But take a situation in which one's place of business dictated what one did for at least eight hours a day. Add to that a housewife who never did plan very well, and you come up with two people at sea. Drift will inevitably set in unless something is done about the situation. And, while we're at it, I think it is safe to say that no one ever drifts into righteousness. That is not the direction that the world is flowing. Once one steps into the drift of this world, he will be carried along by a stream that leads to chaos, confusion and sin.

It is therefore essential to counsel elderly Christians to plan and schedule their days, and then perform accordingly. If you are not the brother who comes alongside to share in the problem in order to enable the counselee to continue on his own (Galatians 6:5), then you will fail in your responsibility to him. When you see disorganization, chaotic conditions, and the like, you, as a counselor, will want to know the reason behind them. Sometimes those conditions will be the result of the waning physical abilities of those who are creating the mess. In these sorts of circumstances you should be concerned to inform and involve family members. If they are not available, or (sadly) are uninterested, then you may need to enlist members of the eld-

erly[1] believer's church to help. It is not healthy for them to continue living in such conditions. They may tell you that they like
it that way (out of pride, despair or sheer lethargy) but down
underneath they probably do not.

God made man not only to be a working creature, but to be
one who would do so efficiently. We know that man is made in
the image of the God Who plans His work and then works His
plan. When Jesus came into this world He did so according to a
divine timetable that was spelled out in Daniel 9. His death
occurred at the very half year specified in that chapter. The
events of Isaiah 53 occurred exactly as planned, and Peter made
the point in his sermons to the Jews that everything happened
precisely as was predestinated (Cf. Acts 2:23; 3:18; 4:27, 28).
All prophecy presupposes planning. When He appeared in the
fullness of time, Jesus knew He was operating on a schedule.
Scripture speaks about **His hour** which at one point had not yet
come (John 7:30; 8:20). Then, when time had run out and the
cross was at hand, He spoke of it as finally having **come** (John
12:23; 17:1).

If God works according to a plan and schedule, and if Jesus'
ministry was scheduled down to the hour of His death, then it is
important to see that human beings, created in God's image, cannot function well apart from planning. Yet, because of the fact
that their time is no longer structured by others, many elderly
saints try to function without any plans or schedules. They just
take things as they come; in other words, they live by drift. They
may tell you that's the way they like it ("it avoids unnecessary
pressure," etc.) but that probably isn't true. Lack of planning is
what creates unnecessary pressure—one never knows when
what might take place. That keeps everyone and everything up in
the air. Suspense and guesswork are not easy to live with. Perhaps more than we recognize, older people have trouble because

---

[1] Perhaps some from the OFCM will do so.

of their lack of disciplined living. Paul talked about lack of structure in II Thessalonians 3:11-13. Because of the **unstructured
way** in which they were living some of the Thessalonians were
idly going about doing little (v. 7) but minding others' business
and failing to assume their own responsibilities (I Thessalonians
4:11, 12). This is often a problem associated with older persons
as well. This problem of idleness was so serious that Paul suggested the possible need for church discipline if it was not corrected (II Thessalonians 3:14, 15).

It should be clear, then, that clutter, chaos and confusion are
not God's ways. Therefore they are not to be the ways of His
children. If the clutter comes from the accumulation of things no
longer useful to one in his old age, he should sell or give away
those things to someone who could use them. There may be a
young couple whom he knows at church starting out marriage
with very little who could be greatly helped by such gifts. Here
the problem is not only planning, but also the failure to let go of
things that are no longer of real use.

"OK, so planning isn't only for the young; it is important for
older Christians as well. How do you help them do this?" Well,
to begin with, you may have to convince them biblically. It isn't
enough simply to set forth the practical advantages that will
accrue. We are not to be pragmatists. The biblical material developed briefly above should be a good starting point. You will
need to take the time to spread this out before them.

Then, presuming that at length you have succeeded in con-
vincing them that this is the biblical course to take, you may
have to show them how to plan. That is true especially if they
have never done much planning in the past. If, on the other hand,
they were good planners before, you might simply ask them how
they would go about organizing their lives for the future. If they
seem to have a pretty good idea about what to do, you might turn
them loose and later check out what they have done, adding to or
correcting their written plans as the case may be. That will be the

simplest approach. However, there will be times (perhaps more than you would want) when you must begin at the beginning and explain all sorts of matters that have to do with planning and scheduling.

One preliminary matter: you too must be a structured, disciplined person who knows how to plan and schedule, and who regularly does so in his own life. If you have problems of your own, don't even try to help others until you have solved them. You will only bring more confusion into their homes.

Where do you begin? Each case will differ somewhat, of course. In one, clutter is a large problem; in another, that doesn't even enter into the equation. So, with the help of the elderly person or persons involved, you must begin by *assessing* the situation. Ask yourself (and them) what problem(s) must be resolved? Having laid these out, defined them clearly and put them in the order of importance, begin to sketch out a plan for dealing with each of them. The "order of importance" may stem from any number of matters. If in one case clutter, for instance, is keeping the counselee(s) from achieving much else, it may be of prime importance. If watching TV all day and late into the night is the sin that is keeping a counselee from achieving what is worthwhile, then that must be dealt with first. So, you must address what seems primary. You cannot build until you have laid the foundation. What in each case is foundational to everything else? Is there something? Perhaps not. There may be a host of little things that, conglomerated, make up a large mess. So assess the situation carefully before you attempt to do anything else.

Next, having determined what must be done, try to place the matters on a schedule that you help the counselee(s) to draw up. In other words, you are teaching him to plan by planning with him what sort of plan he needs to develop and follow in learning to plan!

Then, *tackle* the plan. Work out times (realistic ones) for the beginning and the completion of each task that is involved. Set the dates for these. At some point, perhaps, you might be discussing the scheduling of regular Bible study. You discover that the couple you are counseling doesn't even know how to study the Bible. No one ever taught them; they never took the initiative to ask for instruction. Well, why set out a course of Bible study before they know how to do it? You are setting them up for failure. They may not have many more years to study; you will want those years to be as valuable and productive as possible. So, having assessed that situation, you first tell them to buy a copy of *What to do on Thursday,* a book that teaches the practical use of the Scriptures. Having launched them on that (spending so much time at a particular, agreed upon time each day[1]), in time you will move to the next item on your list. And so on and on.

If you are doing this kind of counseling, you will want to give assignments all along that step up the process of change. People who catch on, who recognize the benefit of living by structure, and who are anxious to move ahead more rapidly will not appreciate your dragging your feet. But be sure that you are getting results when you do. Don't move ahead until you are sure about the person(s) involved. Are they actually achieving past tasks? They may be willing to settle for slipshod work; you should not. They may be anxious to progress, but they may also want to bite off more than they can chew. All of these judgments are an important part of counseling. It is critical that they seek wisdom to make judgments on their own by the study of the Bible and prayer. Having and using biblical wisdom honors God.

Finally, after laying out the plan, you must encourage the counselee(s) *to commit* to and stick to it. You should explicitly

---

[1] You will, of course, check up to make sure they are 1) actually doing the study; 2) doing it rightly. Assuming too much may be fatal to genuine achievement.

call for commitment. But be sure that the counselee knows what the commitment will mean.

The word *commitment* is used all the time in Christian circles, but seldom explained. It seems that true commitment involves at least five factors. These are:

1. *Knowing* what one is getting into. Otherwise the project is too vague to agree to do.

2. *Desiring* to do it. Not necessarily because the task is pleasant, but because one wishes to please God.

3. *Having* the skills and resources to accomplish a task. Or, if necessary, obtaining them.

4. *Scheduling* the activity.

5. *Following* through by keeping to the schedule.

As you can see, each of these five factors is vital to a true commitment that you can expect to get results from. On one hand, one may *want* to do something; but when he really looks into it fully, he discovers that it was very different than what he thought. Desire without knowledge almost always leads to failure. Until he commits to something clear and explicit, his commitment will be shaky. On the other hand, he may know what the task involves, but he may not be properly motivated to do it. Until he sees that it is something that his Lord requires, and he therefore determines to do it (however unpleasant or difficult it may be) because he wants to please Him, he probably will not do it. Or he may have a good understanding of the project, really want to do it, but possess none of the skills to pull it off. "Commitment" of that sort is futile. He must acquire the skills and resources. Then, with all of the above in line, if he doesn't schedule it—first, second, third—attaching times and dates to each element, there is a good chance that the project will never become a reality. Finally, even if all four items are in place, and a wonderful plan complete with schedule has been sketched out, nothing is going to happen if the plan isn't followed. When attempting to teach others about planning and scheduling, I suggest that you go through the five points above, checking off each to make sure genuine commitment is understood.[1] In other words, you need a commitment to true commitment—not just words or intentions that all seem good.

So, in helping counselees up in age plan and schedule their lives you want to make it clear that these efforts are in order to help them please God, settle down, relax and have an easier life while serving Christ effectively. Scheduling does not really bind one. It is chaos that does. When you have an item on your schedule you may look at it and tell someone who asks you to do something else on that day and at that time that you cannot. And you may do so with a good conscience. If you say "no" when you aren't sure that you might or might not have the time, you will feel uneasy about the reply (the same is true if you say "yes"). Scheduling gives confidence and settles one down.

About the only time when you disregard your schedule and place another item in the same block as something you previously scheduled is when you can find an equally good spot to which to move the scheduled item. Again, you have no difficulty doing this since your calendar will inform you whether or not there is an equally good block to which to move it. Without a schedule you might create more confusion and guilt if you do so.

One other instance when a counselee will want to take a hard look at his schedule is when large changes occur. A schedule that fits one circumstance will not always be appropriate to another. If there is a death of one of the parties in a marriage, a relocation of one's living place, etc., it will be necessary to reappraise previously laid plans and schedules. In all cases, it might be important to review the schedule quarterly to make sure that even if no

---

[1] It might be valuable to print these five items on a card that you give to counselees who must make commitments. Also be careful to make a point of observing that all commitments are made to the Lord, not to you. It matters little whether you are pleased or not; it matters much whether He is.

large changes have occurred there has not been an accumulation of smaller ones that is equal a larger one.

I doubt that many have thought about the scheduling of the elderly since there has been so much emphasis on leisure time. Scheduling doesn't eliminate the leisure that is needed for R&R as that applies to older people who must rest and relax more than they did previously, but it does help them not to fritter away the remainder of their days. Rest and leisure ought also be scheduled. In combination with a ministry of some sort planning and scheduling makes it possible to get things done. Indeed, all the things that I have been advocating throughout this book coordinate with one another. Like the old song said, "You can't have the one without the other." It is because there are those who try to accept some of the pieces of the whole and not the others that they fail. I have been advocating a *lifestyle*, the pieces of which all go together to make a whole. It is a lifestyle that, with many adjustments for particular situations, in all cases attempts to make the remaining years of one's life productive, useful times of growing and serving that bring about true happiness and make the hope of eternal life a reality. I urge you to help counselees to get on board.

Chapter Twelve

Introspection

Introspection may be good or bad. All the word means is looking inside. Why you look inside, how you look inside, what you find when you do and what you do about it makes all the difference.

If one engages in introspection merely to dredge up some old experiences, complete with moss and mold, then introspection hardly can be said to be of help to an older counselee. If he only broods on them in a spirit that has no better purpose in view, he is thereby likely to hatch a nest full of discouragements. You'd think that no one would want to do this; but there is an innumerable host of morbid souls who seem to delight in mucking up memories from the past simply for the purpose of groveling in them. Their latter days are filled with regrets over what they have done and what others have done to them. They spend hours picking through the rubble of a life poorly lived, feeling sorry for themselves and getting more and more bitter about others. That is hardly the way for anyone—let alone a Christian—to live out the remainder of his days. There is precedent in many Psalms for looking back and remembering the goodness and the mercies of the Lord that have been showered upon him. There is profit in thinking about the ways in which others have been a blessing to you. But wasting valuable time in sordid introspection to see where you went wrong in choosing friends, pursuing certain courses of life and making decisions? Unh, uh! There is nothing Christian about that.

Well, then, how can introspection be good? Introspection is good and useful to a counselee when it leads to productive activity. Sure, there is plenty that we have done wrong. Certainly there are actions that every sinner regrets. Of course, there are things we might have done differently. There are people who have wronged us. And it is not wrong to think back in order to dredge some of this up *if* —and it is a big *if*—counselees do so for the purpose of rectifying as many of those situations as possible. *If* they wish to learn from the past so as to change in the future and *if* they are interested in clearing their relationship with God because of some guilt it can be profitable.

The key to proper introspection is doing so *in the light of biblical principles.* If one simply looks inside and tries to do something about what he finds there that troubles him, more than likely that approach will lead to additional words or actions that he may live to regret. He must examine himself according to biblical categories or 1) he will reach wrong conclusions, 2) he will make wrong judgments about himself and others and 3) he will adopt wrong solutions to problems. All introspection, to be helpful rather than harmful, must be biblically guided.

So what should you help him to do? You might ask him various questions to stimulate good introspection and to guide it along certain lines. Here are a couple (though each response will probably lead to further questions unique to each situation):

1. Is there anyone to whom you owe anything?
2. Is there anyone to whom you should grant forgiveness?[1]
3. Is there anyone you need to confront about a wrong?
4. Is there anything between God and you that you need to confess?

Questions like this should trigger discussions between him and yourself. You should make sure that these discussions lead to action on the part of the counselee. How wonderful to be able to

---

[1] You may need to develop this according to discussions in my book *From forgiven to Forgiving.*

bring about reconciliation between brothers before it is too late to do so! Surely, you want to see that this happens, don't you? Then you must screw up the courage to ask questions like that to help counselees engage in helpful introspection.

How can you detect the need for someone to do some good introspection? Well, one sign may be the fact that his morale is very low. He has lost the brightness that he exhibited in former visits. Now, that could be the result of new medication, or some other extraneous factor. But if he keeps talking about sad events in the past or persons with whom there has been difficulty, you may be fairly sure that he has already been doing some introspection—but usually of the wrong kind! You want him to look at such events and relationships from a biblical viewpoint to determine whether something needs to be done to clear up problems that have never been properly dealt with. Your concern is for him to turn the introspection into a means of sanctification, thereby honoring God. As a result, his morale should also improve.

If a person has been engaging in introspection that leads to nothing more than worse attitudes and lower morale, you should not let him continue to do so without addressing the problem. If you fail to do so, your counselee may slide deeper and deeper inside of himself until he has become virtually disengaged with those around him. Your concern, remember, is to help him to live out a vital Christian life in his latter days. If you want him to go into eternity praising and thanking God, having accomplished much even in his later years, you will not avoid dealing with counselees whose morale is low.

There are many things about the past that everyone can recall if he digs deeply enough and long enough that are of no present consequence. You are not to encourage the making of exhaustive lists of things only half remembered. That isn't what I have in mind. But there may be matters that happened in the past that are of present concern. Those are not really past events only. Once a man spoke to me about something that had burdened his heart for years. He had vacillated as to whether or not he should speak about it for almost as many years. Finally, when he was a year or so away from death, he spoke. He had burned down a store half a century ago to collect insurance money. He had gotten away with it so far as the insurance company was concerned and so far as the law knew. But *he* remembered! And it had plagued him for 50 years. Only when he coughed it up and received the advice to deal with it before God and to make restitution did he find relief. That is the sort of introspection that is profitable.

Introspection for introspection's sake is harmful. For one thing, if it becomes overwhelming, occupying a great deal of time every day, one becomes involved in a process of regression; he is going in the wrong direction. He is living his life backward! Every Christian should be forward looking and living. Looking at the immediate future and the ultimate future, he should live the former in the light of the latter. The only useful purpose for introspection, therefore, is to clear up the rubble of the past so as to get on with the future. The goal is to put the past where it belongs—in the past. So, one is not problem-oriented in the introspection, but is solution-oriented. Poking about in the rubble of past destructive events simply to see what one can turn up is unprofitable and, if persisted in, can be sinful.[1]

Ask yourself, "How often have I detected signs of harmful introspection in counselees and have done nothing about it?" If you reflect (introspectively, in a biblically, solution-oriented mode), doubtless you will come up with some incidents and emerge with a determination never to allow that to happen again. Now that determination, if combined with commitment (see the last chapter), is the sort of thing that good introspection can achieve.

---

[1] It is like returning to the scene of the crime!

Proper introspection also may lead to the remembrance of good things others and God have done and, out of growing gratitude, may spur one on to even greater activity in old age. His remembering the serious illness from which God healed him, the automobile accident from which he walked away alive, the time when his children held a really special 50th anniversary party for him and his wife—these and dozens of other pleasant memories ought to cause gratitude and thanksgiving to well up within him. A certain tenderness may develop that will melt down some of the harsher aspects of old age. Oldsters have a long period of time to reflect on. But they must not merely reminisce. You must not allow a counselee to wallow in miseries or bask in pleasant memories without commenting about it. Introspection ought all to be harnessed in order to put some horsepower into his present activities of living before God, his neighbors and his family.

Psalm 18 is David's longest. It is a trip into the past that occasions the gratitude and praise that is expressed in the introductory verses 1-3. David then catalogs God's blessings culled from his memories of the past and leading to his concluding affirmations in verses 46 through 50. In this Psalm David names himself (v. 50). Naming himself probably indicates that in a special way he wanted to thank God for His many mercies in the past. At any rate, the Psalm is the result of highly reflective thought—thought very close to what we have called good introspection. Here is Psalm 18:

1 **"I love You, O LORD, my strength."**
2 **The LORD is my rock and my fortress and my deliverer,
My God, my rock, in whom I take refuge;
My shield and the horn of my salvation, my stronghold.**
3 **I call upon the LORD, who is worthy to be praised,
And I am saved from my enemies.**

4 **The cords of death encompassed me,
And the torrents of ungodliness terrified me.**

5   The cords of Sheol surrounded me;
     The snares of death confronted me.

6   In my distress I called upon the LORD,
     And cried to my God for help;
     He heard my voice out of His temple,
     And my cry for help before Him came into His ears.

7   Then the earth shook and quaked;
     And the foundations of the mountains were trembling
     And were shaken, because He was angry.

8   Smoke went up out of His nostrils,
     And fire from His mouth devoured;
     Coals were kindled by it.

9   He bowed the heavens also, and came down
     With thick darkness under His feet.

10 He rode upon a cherub and flew;
     And He sped upon the wings of the wind.

11 He made darkness His hiding place, His canopy around
     Him,
     Darkness of waters, thick clouds of the skies.

12 From the brightness before Him passed His thick
     clouds,
     Hailstones and coals of fire.

13 The LORD also thundered in the heavens,
     And the Most High uttered His voice,
     Hailstones and coals of fire.

14 He sent out His arrows, and scattered them,
     And lightning flashes in abundance, and routed them.

15 Then the channels of water appeared,
     And the foundations of the world were laid bare
     At Your rebuke, O LORD,
     At the blast of the breath of Your nostrils.

16 He sent from on high, He took me;
     He drew me out of many waters.

17 He delivered me from my strong enemy,
     And from those who hated me, for they were too mighty
     for me.

18 They confronted me in the day of my calamity,
But the LORD was my stay.
19 He brought me forth also into a broad place;
He rescued me, because He delighted in me.

20 The LORD has rewarded me according to my
righteousness;
According to the cleanness of my hands He has
recompensed me.
21 For I have kept the ways of the LORD,
And have not wickedly departed from my God.
22 For all His ordinances were before me,
And I did not put away His statutes from me.
23 I was also blameless with Him,
And I kept myself from my iniquity.
24 Therefore the LORD has recompensed me according to
my righteousness,
According to the cleanness of my hands in His eyes.

25 With the kind You show Yourself kind;
With the blameless You show Yourself blameless;
26 With the pure You show Yourself pure,
And with the crooked You show Yourself astute.
27 For You save an afflicted people,
But haughty eyes You abase.
28 For You light my lamp;
The LORD my God illumines my darkness.
29 For by You I can run upon a troop;
And by my God I can leap over a wall.

30 As for God, His way is blameless;
The word of the LORD is tried;
He is a shield to all who take refuge in Him.
31 For who is God, but the LORD?
And who is a rock, except our God,
32 The God who girds me with strength
And makes my way blameless?
33 He makes my feet like hinds' *feet*,
And sets me upon my high places.

34 **He trains my hands for battle,**
     So that my arms can bend a bow of bronze.
35 **You have also given me the shield of Your salvation,**
     And Your right hand upholds me;
     And Your gentleness makes me great.
36 **You enlarge my steps under me,**
     And my feet have not slipped.

37 **I pursued my enemies and overtook them,**
     And I did not turn back until they were consumed.
38 **I shattered them, so that they were not able to rise;**
     They fell under my feet.
39 **For You have girded me with strength for battle;**
     You have subdued under me those who rose up against
       me.
40 **You have also made my enemies turn their backs to me,**
     And I destroyed those who hated me.
41 **They cried for help, but there was none to save,**
     ***Even* to the LORD, but He did not answer them.**
42 **Then I beat them fine as the dust before the wind;**
     I emptied them out as the mire of the streets.

43 **You have delivered me from the contentions of the**
       people;
     You have placed me as head of the nations;
     A people whom I have not known serve me.
44 **As soon as they hear, they obey me;**
     Foreigners submit to me.
45 **Foreigners fade away,**
     And come trembling out of their fortresses.

46 **The LORD lives, and blessed be my rock;**
     And exalted be the God of my salvation,
47 **The God who executes vengeance for me,**
     And subdues peoples under me.
48 **He delivers me from my enemies;**
     Surely You lift me above those who rise up against me;
     You rescue me from the violent man.

49 **Therefore I will give thanks to You among the nations,**
   O LORD,
   And I will sing praises to Your name.
50 **He gives great deliverance to His king,**
   And shows lovingkindness to His anointed,
   To David and his descendants forever.

Now that's introspection using retrospection in order to pass inspection before God!

Chapter Thirteen

Complaining

To adapt the wording of Matthew 18, "Where two or three older people are gathered together, there in the midst is someone complaining." They may be complaining about the high cost of food, about lumbago or gout, about how the government doesn't pay enough attention to the needs of the elderly, or—you name it! Complaints! Complaints! Complaints! They seem to go with the territory.

Must older people engage in so much complaining? Do their conversations have to deteriorate into "can you top this" matches? Can't people—Christian older people especially—grow old gracefully? Of course they can; and some do. But there is too much complaining going on. If one is bent on complaining, he will soon find that there is plenty to complain about in a world of sin. And it is even easier to find things to complain about when one grows older. All of the losses mentioned earlier in this book added to the normal difficulties people of all ages experience provide more than enough ammunition if one is looking for it. But, of course, that is the key: *if he is looking for it.*

It is just as true that the believer *who is looking for it* can as readily discover the good hand of God at work. So in the end, complaining and thankful people have two different orientations that two different attitudes have produced in them. These attitudes, in turn, come from two distinct views of life (doctrines of providence). The one view/attitude is virtually atheistic (a believer can at times think and act like an atheist) and the other is theistic to the core. However, the one with the theistic view thinks of all that happens in God's universe as part of His providential working in order to bring about good in accordance with His promise in Romans 8:28 and 29. The other forgets God in daily living and carries on as if things that occur just do so by chance. When he complains about the weather, it is just the weather that has come; for him it is not that God sends the clouds and the rain for His beneficent purposes. When a "tragedy" occurs, he can see nothing beyond the tragic dimensions of the event. It doesn't even occur to him to think about what purposes God may have in it or that God is behind the event.[1] Consequently, he complains.

But if this truly is God's world, if He truly is in control of all events and is guiding not only the course of world history but also the personal histories of each individual, when one complains about his circumstances that means he is *complaining about God's ways and God's providence*. And that is serious business!

The people of God complained in the desert and, we read, **with most of them God was displeased and their bodies were scattered over the desert** (I Corinthians 10:5). The **grumbling** of which Paul speaks in verse 8 led to the death of 23,000 people **in a single day** (cf. also v. 10)! God did not treat lightly the complaints of His people. When they complained about the manna, He responded by sending so much quail that it practically came out of their ears! When they complained about Moses' taking so long to come down from the mountain, and they began to worship a golden calf, God was extremely displeased and sent fiery serpents into their midst.

Why did God respond so strongly to their complaints? Because, at bottom all complaints are complaints against Him. God had these events and His response to them recorded for the Corinthians (and your counselee) who would live at a much later date, but who would need to hear His word about grumbling,

---

[1] I cannot enter into a discussion of the problem of evil here. But I have done so in my book, *The Grand Demonstration (q.v.)*.

grousing and complaining (vv. 6, 10, 11). Perhaps a grumbling older counselee needs to hear you read the first 13 verses of I Corinthians 10 to him. The chapter ought always be in your mind when you visit with older persons.

So how can one change and become a thankful, grateful, praising person, instead of a grump? That is what you must help him do. It is possible because God tells your grumpy counselee to learn from the experience of those in the wilderness and from Paul's writing to the Corinthians. God never requires anything of His children that He doesn't give both the direction and the power to accomplish. Take heart counselor. Tell your counselee to take heart too.

But first, you must convince him that complaining is wrong. I have taken the time to mention I Corinthians 10 so that you will have a starting point with which to address a complaining older counselee. You probably will need to convince him that complaining is sin. How do we know that? Because God commands him not to grumble. Disobedience to God is sin. He makes it clear that all complaints are really complaints about Him and His providence. To complain to God about how He is running His universe surely is sin!

Moreover, complaining leads to idolatry. When one rejects the ways of God, he always turns to some other way. They grumbled, and the next thing you saw—they were worshipping a God of their own making. And in connection with idolatry, they became involved in lewd behavior. Complaining, then, isn't all that innocuous after all. It keeps bad company! Make that clear.

So, the first thing you must do in helping an older person, who may have developed the habit of complaining way back in his youth, is to convince him that complaining is sin and that it must be replaced with an entirely different lifestyle. This passage in I Corinthians 10 is pivotal for doing so.

Next, you will want to show him that God takes complaining seriously. Make a note of the fact that He destroyed an entire generation of His people for that sin. You cannot threaten that God will take away his life before his time, but you can tell your counselee that God has done so in the past, and there is certainly no reason why He will not do so when it suits His purposes today. But of greatest importance, tell him that if he is grateful for his salvation, he ought to want to please God. And obviously, complaining about what He is doing doesn't do so. That, not the threat of death, is the better motive from which to act. But the Bible uses all sorts of motives in appealing to sinning believers who have closed their ears to God's servants.

Assuming that one confesses his sin of complaining, what happens next? He may protest, "This is a long standing habit, and though I now want to shake it, I find it difficult to do so. Before I know it, I have not only found something to complain about, but the complaint itself slips out of my mouth. Then, I have to confess and ask forgiveness for it. How can I get past the problem?"

When your counselee is talking like that, half the battle is won. Tell him that change is not always easy, but that it can be done. First, it is not merely a matter of "shaking off" an old habit. That, of course, must happen. But you may never merely break a habit; you must *replace* it. And you replace it with the biblical alternative. Instead of a sour, unpleasant life of gripes and complaints, you want to develop a joyful, inviting life of praise and thanksgiving. That is the biblical alternative. To do so, one must be thoroughly convinced of the fact that God **works all things together for good** for His children who love Him. If that is so, then one ought not to look primarily on the difficult or even tragic side of an event. Rather, he ought to search out the good in it.[1] Now, neither every goal that God has in the event, nor every good that He is bringing about by it will necessarily become apparent immediately. Sometimes it may take months or even

---

[1] One good that is always present is to help him become more like Christ (cf. v. 29).

years to get some perspective on it and see how it worked for good. At other times, it will not be until the effects of the event have run their course that he can begin to understand God's good ways in it. Then, there are times when the counselee will never in this lifetime be able to determine what good will come out of the event. Usually, however, at least some good will begin to appear soon after an event. But if one doesn't have the eyes to see or the heart to understand, he is likely to miss it. Attitude is all-important in the search. So, to develop a new approach to life, one must purposely begin to look for the good hand of God at work in every happening.

How does one do that? He does three things. First, when it occurs, he immediately says to himself, "Now, I know God is in the event. It didn't just happen. It happened because God wanted it to happen." That is to say, he exchanges the atheistic attitude that I mentioned above for a theistic one in which God is sovereign. To see God in every event changes everything. It means that it has meaning. Events—even sad ones—can become an adventure with God. Next, he says, "God is up to something in the event. It didn't just happen. It happened for some purpose(s)." So, he begins to search out as much of that purpose as he can. Lastly, he says, "God is up to something good in this. It didn't just happen. It happened because God had some good result(s) in mind." He then searches out whatever good he can find in the event.

Help counselees to consciously work on doing this. They will not find that overnight the new way will replace the old. Counseling experience has revealed that it usually takes about forty days and forty nights of disciplined, regular practice to establish a new habit in the place of an old one. People who fail usually do so because they are impatient. They do not want to work and wait that long. They want instant change. But apart from some immediate work of God, change is rarely instantaneous. Human beings have been given natures that work in the way they were designed to work. Human nature takes time and effort to change. So, counselor, stick with them. Encourage them all along the way. If and when a counselee slips back or gives up, work with him until once again he is back at work, prayerfully putting off the old ways and putting on the new ones (cf. Proverbs 24:16).

Now, as he goes along learning the new way, he will want to begin to tell others of those good things that he has been discovering in events. Instead of complaining, he will find himself saying things such as, "You know, that really was a remarkable event. God's good hand was surely in it, don't you think?" Then, when someone asks, "How is that?" Having searched it out he can say, "Well, I noticed that . . . ." He has begun a life of thanksgiving and praise.

One other activity will soon emerge as well. He will be praying in a new and more thankful way. His prayers will take on a much more positive note. And as his prayers change, his attitude will change. As his attitude changes, his prayers will change. It is cyclical. Along with that, his theology will become enriched and he will begin to have greater insight into the ways of God with His world. Doubtless he will be reading his Bible in a new light. He will search its pages for ways in which God brought good out of evil, making even the wrath of man to praise Him. He will want to find clues about discerning the hand of God in providence. And as he does, his theology will be enriched all the more, his prayers will take on new hues, his attitude will improve, and he will be developing a new lifestyle cycling upward in praise and gratitude.

So, wizened old grouches can change! It is about time, at that age, don't you think? You better believe it. No one is ever too old to change if he is willing to do so. Always keep that hope alive in your own heart. Light and fan the flame in the hearts of your counselees as well. There are few things more sad (and reprehensible) than meeting an elderly Christian who is sour about life. There are few things more invigorating than meeting one who is genuinely full of praise and thanksgiving.[1] So, counselor, do what you can to bring about the latter in the lives of the former. That is a great and challenging counseling task!

---

[1] There are those who pretend. I'm talking about reality.

Chapter Fourteen

Doctrinal Problems

So far in this book I have mentioned only one doctrinal error—the error of thinking that one who is saved could be lost once more. As I indicated in that place, this error takes away hope because it sets one out on the hopeless course of *keeping* himself saved. Salvation would not be the work of Christ then, but the work of Christ *and* the believer. But if in any sense whatever salvation depends on what I have to do, there is no hope for me. I would be the weak link in the chain. Such poor doctrine is bound to encourage poor introspection, discouragement and, ultimately, despair. All error has deleterious effects.

Doctrine always influences life—for good or for ill (cf. Titus 1:1). That is why every counselor must be prepared at all times to discuss doctrine.[1] He cannot avoid doctrine and think that he can counsel biblically. Many of the sinful life patterns that are recognized in the New Testament are inextricably linked with false teaching. So, it is incumbent upon every counselor of the elderly to be ready to confront error whenever he encounters it so as to help his counselees spend the remainder of their lives in truth, enjoying the peace and confidence that it brings. False doctrine brings confusion, fear, doubt and despair.

There are other doctrinal teachings abroad that trouble the lives of older persons (as well as those of the younger[2]). Take, for instance, the doctrine of instant sanctification. The essence of this teaching in its many forms is that by some process (usually a

---

[1] Of course, that means he must be well informed doctrinally.

[2] But they are particularly troublesome to elderly Christians who have fol-

series of steps) a person may attain a state either of sinless perfection or near perfection (at the very least, a "higher life" than the rest of us peons in the church experience). According to this quietistic doctrine,[1] the "cloud nine" experience may be attained by "yielding," or "letting go and letting God," or something equivalent.

The truth of the matter is that sanctification is progressive, not instantaneous. One must gradually *grow* **in** [or by] **grace** (II Peter 3:18). Growth is never instantaneous. Never in addressing the many sins mentioned in the New Testament do you find a writer advising any sort of act or series of acts that supposedly will impart instant victory over them. Always, instead, the kind of teaching that is found in Ephesians 4 (and the parallel passage in Colossians) is set forth as the solution to the problem—putting off the old lifestyle more and more as one is putting on the new lifestyle. The quietistic error fundamentally lies in the confusion of justification with sanctification. In justification, one is *considered* perfect by faith. That is, instantaneously, the perfect righteousness of Christ is attributed or reckoned to him. In sanctification, however, one gradually becomes in actuality more and more what he is accounted to be in the books of heaven. We must never substitute the essential Roman Catholic doctrine of infusion of righteousness for the biblical doctrine of the imputation of righteousness.

Those who hold to the instantaneous sanctification doctrine can only despair after a time. After all, in old age there are enough trials (physical and otherwise) to bring out the fact that there is much sin remaining in a believer, and that he has by no

---

lowed them for years thinking that they could achieve the promised effects in their lives only to discover that they have failed. Think of going through life expecting God to do things that He has never told you to expect. The result? Serious doubts about the faith or about one's self.

[1] Quietism means that one expects God to do something *for* him *instead of* him. The truth is that God sanctifies as the believer obeys His Word.

means achieved perfection—or even "life on a higher plane" than other Christians. Only if he is blinded to reality, is extremely egotistical, or avoids introspection altogether could he ever conclude that he has reached "cloud nine." In addition, the realization that for years he has failed to reach the goal of entire sanctification, and now that his life is drawing to a close he still has not "yielded all,"[1] can only bring about discouragement and confusion. If he doesn't conclude that he is yet unsaved, he is most likely to think that he must strive harder to strive less![2]

Another harmful false doctrine that may affect the life of your elderly counselee for ill is the doctrine that he can know the time of Christ's second coming. There are any number of older persons who, because they would like to escape death, will tell you that they are sure that Christ will return soon—this year, perhaps, and possibly (note their eyes light up at this) in their lifetime. They will spend inordinate amounts of time trying to figure out the "prophetic signs" that supposedly announce Jesus' coming.[3] They will run from one prophetic teacher to another. They will waste great gobs of resources and time reading, studying and speculating about the issue. The motivation, as you may readily ascertain from them, is that they want to be raptured before death.

Once more, we may see how the erroneous idea that one may know the time of Christ's return may wreak havoc in the lives of elderly counselees. It may lead to a sort of desperation to stay alive when it looks like the remaining time before their departure

---

[1] Phrases like the following are particularly troublesome: "If Jesus isn't Lord of all, He isn't Lord at all." If what that phrase expresses was a biblical truth, it would mean that no one has Christ as Lord.

[2] This is the fundamental frustration of quietism. It's like saying, "I must work harder at relaxing." At its core is contradiction.

[3] And, if they arrive at a set time, they may make foolish moves in preparation for it (selling all and giving proceeds to some prophetic teacher, etc.). Cf. I Timothy 1:3-7.

to be with Christ is drawing to a close. And the worst thing about it all is that you hear otherwise biblical preachers and others irresponsibly saying things like: "Well, the way things are today in the country, I don't see how the second coming can be much farther off." Such talk is irresponsible because there is no way of setting dates. And it only encourages older persons who fear death to become preoccupied with vain speculations.

Now, there will be a generation of believers who will not see death when Christ returns. Nevertheless, every Christian must prepare for death. He cannot know the time Christ will come since God has held that date close to His chest. It will be wonderful for those saints who are alive to meet Him in the air to escort Him in His descent when He returns, but there is no way anyone can know if he is to be a part of that privileged generation. And, the passages to which these persons usually refer actually have little or nothing to do with the time of Christ's return[1] (cf. my commentary on Matthew; especially chapter 24[2]).

Another false teaching that may affect your elderly counselee is the idea that illness is entirely the result of a lack of faith. There are those who teach that there is no sickness that God will not heal if one has faith. I have addressed this briefly in a previous chapter of this book, but I must say how utterly devastating that doctrine can be to a sick older person! It may tear him up as he thinks that he has exercised the requisite faith yet finds no healing, and the confusion and doubt occasioned thereby only exacerbate the sickness itself. Some may begin to question God's promises. Elderly persons who are suffering from some infirmity need encouragement and help; they don't need other problems heaped upon those they already are experiencing. Be sure to disabuse the elderly of all such false ideas.

---

[1] Actually, the verses usually appealed to teach just the opposite—that **the end is not yet**.

[2] In the *Christian Counselor's Commentary*.

And while it isn't exactly set forth as a doctrine, many elderly people hold to a belief that if and when their spouse dies, they will move to Florida (California, Arizona, Nevada, etc.) and live the remainder of their lives in sunny ease. Sometimes it works out that way. More often it does not. Locations do not themselves make a change in a person. Wherever he goes, he takes himself along—together with all of his troubles and sins. Moreover, he also leaves his old surroundings behind. He may leave church, family and/or friends. In the new place, he finds it very difficult to develop new friendships with peers. Before you know it, he is longing to be back "home" again. But it is too late. He has sold all and invested (often poorly) in housing and other things, in the sunshine land. As a counselor of the elderly, advise those who have recently lost loved ones to make no immediate great changes. That means that they should not make large expenditures, decisions to sell or move, take a cruise around the world, or the like. Urge them to get perspective on things before making any radical decisions; usually, they should wait six months or so. There is enough change to get used to after the loss of a loved one. To deliberately throw new and unnecessary changes (that usually turn out to be more losses) into the equation will only deepen the original loss! Wise counsel from one's pastor to this effect will be greatly appreciated a year or so down the pike.

I could go on mentioning false doctrines that have caused older persons untold heartache and despair. But I shall add only one more. It is the idea of having "missed out on God's perfect will." Those who hold to this doctrine teach that one may have lived all his life at a sort of secondary or tertiary level because somewhere along the line he got off the main track. Because he failed to see that right switch, that one bad move took him away on another track; there was no way to ever get back on the main one. He was stuck and must remain so, and is now deeply immersed in regrets. Such teaching rips Romans 5:20 out of the Bible.

Since he has done such a superb job of putting this notion to rest, I will not address the problem myself. I will simply recommend Gary Friesen's book *Decision Making and the Will of God*. He has shown that the historic, biblical view has been set aside by many in order to accept a new and erroneous one that causes confusion, sorrow and unnecessary difficulties. Surely no one heading into old age should think that because he has "missed God's perfect will" it is impossible to do anything about it. Instead, you must help him to see that it is never too late to start living as one ought and thereby make up for the losses of earlier years. No Christian need ever despair of being able to do God's will at any stage in his life—he can if he only will.

Chapter Fifteen

The Conclusion of the Matter

At the end of the book of Ecclesiastes we read, **fear God and keep His commandments, because this applies to every person** (12:13). Solomon traversed just about all of life's activities in the book. He has declared everything vanity because there is no permanence to any of it. He has adequately set forth the hopelessness of the unbeliever's existence.

The expression **fear God** is a semi-technical one used throughout the Bible to mean humble trust in Him as the One Who alone saves. It is a way of saying there is nothing and no one else to fear when we place our trustful fear in Him (cf. Matthew 10:28). The idea of keeping God's commandments is the next thing to reckon with. Having been saved by faith in the Lord Jesus Christ, one now should seek to **observe all things that He commands** (Matthew 28:20). So the writer is saying that one must be saved and then obey God; that is the sum of what life is really all about. Nothing else counts if that is not in place. That is what faithful counselors tell older persons. It is tragic if for most of their lives they have lived for the vain and impermanent things that Solomon has dismissed as vain. But it is never too late to rectify the situation. Tell your counselees it is now time (if they haven't before) to straighten out their lives, and place the emphasis on the proper things in life (cf. Matthew 6:19-21, 33[1]). Reit-

---

[1] For a fuller discussion of the contrast between Christian and pagan philosophies of life as they are set forth in Matthew 6, see my *Christian Living in the World.*

erate the significance of Romans 5:20—God is able to make good *abound* far more fully than evil ever did.

Now we come to the part of Ecclesiastes 12:13 that has special significance for elderly Christians. It says that **this applies to every person.** There is some question as to whether the word **this** refers to fearing God and keeping His commandments alone or to all that is written in the book previously. There is no significant difference since after twelve chapters of debunking **life under the sun** (that is, life that is lived for this world only), he sums up all he wants to say by way of contrast in verse 13. These two things, he says, are all that is worthwhile because the way of life they produce alone has permanence and is not in vain. And this conclusion **applies to *every* person**. That is to say, even to the elderly. If ever there was a book for them to ponder, this is it. In spite of the many interpretations of individual portions, and even in some respects of the book as a whole, one message comes through loud and clear. It is the message that nothing is worthwhile except those things that pertain to God and His worship. If anyone ought to be able to take this to heart, it should be elderly Christians from whose hands vain things are daily slipping away. If they never have before, what better time than now for them to come to a realization of the truths of this book and to listen to the conclusion of the whole matter.

What, for the believer, then, is the conclusion of the matter? It is to fear God and keep His commandments. It is your privilege to help others see and appropriate this truth as their own personal conclusion to guide them throughout the rest of their lives.

Other Titles by Dr. Jay Adams
available from your bookstore or
directly from TIMELESS TEXTS
1-800-814-1045

The Christian Counselor's Commentary Series
Dr. Jay E. Adams   all volumes hardback

Vol. 1—I & II Corinthians
Vol. 2—Galatians, Ephesians, Colossians & Philemon
Vol. 3—I & II Timothy and Titus
Vol. 4—Romans, Philippians, and I & II Thessalonians
Vol. 5—Hebrews, James, I & II Peter, and Jude
Vol. 6—Proverbs
Vol. 7—The Gospel of John and the Letters of John and Jesus
Vol. 8—The Gospel of Luke
Vol. 9—The Gospels of Matthew and Mark
Vol. 10—Acts

> This series of commentaries is written in everyday
> English. A must for the layman as well as the Pastor/
> Counselor. Dr. Adams' everyman style of communica-
> tion brings forth these biblical truths in a clear under-
> standable way that typifies his writings. He does not try
> to duplicate the standard, more technical types of com-
> mentaries but supplements them with the implications of
> the text for God-honoring counseling and Christian liv-
> ing.

The Christian Counselor's New Testament
translated by Jay E. Adams

> A special translation by Dr. Adams with extensive foot-
> notes and topical side columns. This Bible was specially
> designed to help the Christian in study as well as coun-
> seling. *The Christian Counselor's New Testament*
> is very user friendly. It leads you through those tough
> counseling topics by using the Margin Notations and
> Notation Index for the topic or related topics. Easily used
> during the counseling session.

Back to the Blackboard—
Design for a Biblical Christian School
by Jay E. Adams   160pp. paperback

With curriculum in the courtroom and parents up in arms, education is in the forefront of discussion in much of America today. Here is a truly provocative book on what qualifies as Christian education. These ideas are also very adaptable for the home schooler.

A Call for Discernment—
Distinguishing Truth from Error in Today's Church
by Jay E. Adams   142pp. paperback

Dr. Adams shows the seriousness of the problem of lack of discernment and the effect on Christian lives. *A Call For Discernment* will help you become a more discerning Christian today.

Christian Living in the World—
by Jay E. Adams   110pp. paperback

Do you know how to live in and relate to the world? Many Christians do not ask. This book shows you. Moreover, it may open up larger dimensions of what the Bible is talking about when it uses the word "world." Questions about "animal rights," environmentalism, and vegetarianism are considered biblically along with temptation by the world, the flesh and the devil. A must for the growing Christian who wants to live for God in this world!

The Christian's Guide to Guidance—
by Jay E. Adams   97 pp. paperback

"What shall I do?" Perhaps that question arises as often as any other among perplexed Christians who want to know God's will about choosing a marriage partner, what career to enter, whether or not to move—or a hundred other issues. Answers are rife; but which are right? Do feelings, promptings, signs, or similar phenomena constitute indications of God's will? Can one know for certain what decisions to make? How does God lead? These and many other such matters are answered according to the Bible. You need to settle these questions if you want to live effectively for Jesus Christ.

Counsel from Psalm 119—
by Jay E. Adams   140pp. paperback

The 119th Psalm is the prayer notebook of a man who solved every problem in life by means of the Bible. In verse after verse he explains how the Scriptures sustained and guided him through all of life's vicissitudes. In this book, Psalm 119 is translated, interpreted and applied to counseling. This unique book will help you to live more surefootedly and to help others do the same.

The Grand Demonstration—
> A Biblical Study of the So-Called Problem of Evil
by Jay E. Adams   119pp. paperback

Why is there sin, rape, disease, war, pain and death in a good God's world? Every Christian asks this question—but rarely receives an answer. Read this book and discover what God Himself says.

The Grand Demonstration penetrates deeply into scriptural teaching regarding the nature of God. Moving into territory others fear to tread, Dr. Adams maintains that a fearless acceptance of biblical truth solves the so-called "problem of evil".

Maintaining the Delicate Balance in Christian Living—
115pp. paperback

Biblical Balance—in a world that's out of kilter, that's tilted toward sin! That's what every Christian needs. But the temptation is to lean toward one sinful extreme or the other. In this book Adams not only shows what it means to maintain your spiritual balance but, in a variety of situations in which it is difficult to do so, demonstrates how you can achieve balance.

Teaching to Observe—The Counselor as Teacher
by Jay E. Adams
131pp. paperback

Here is a book that is long overdue. Carl Rogers convinced a generation of counselors to listen and reflect while insisting that teaching is taboo. Though Rogerianism failed, and is now largely passé, many counselors still hesitate to teach their counselees.

Dr. Adams shows not only that God obligates Christian counselors to teach, but how they may do so in ways that will help counselees both learn and "observe" those things that Christ "commanded" according to Matthew 28:20. He demonstrates clearly, using illustrations to which you will resonate, that effective biblical counseling requires teaching. This book, the only one of its kind, is must reading for every serious Christian.

A Thirst For Wholeness
by Jay E. Adams
143pp. paperback

How healthy is your spiritual integrity? Do your actions speak so loudly that people won't listen? *A Thirst for Wholeness* provides the solution to this common problem. Drawing on the book of James, Dr. Adams concentrates on how you can become a complete Christian from the inside out. As you study the inner dynamics involved in this process, you'll learn how to get your spiritual beliefs and your everyday actions in sync.

What to do on Thursday—

A Layman's Guide to the Practical Use of the Scriptures
by Jay E. Adams   144pp. paperback

> The Bible has the answers, but can you find, understand and apply them? *What to do on Thursday* teaches you how to study and interpret your Bible to answer the questions that arise all week at work, at play, at home, and at school.

> Dr. Adams has written this study to prepare you to meet the challenges of this fast-moving world with decisions that will honor God. The practical use of the Scriptures on an everyday basis is crucial to all of God's people. You can't wait for your pastor to preach a sermon that applies to your need now. *What to do on Thursday* will help you prepare a template of priorities that will order your life in a Godly pattern.

Winning the War Within—

A Biblical Strategy for Spiritual Warfare
by Jay E. Adams   151pp. paperback

> Christian, you are at war! It is the battles at two levels—one outward, the other inward—that are our responsibilities as members of the church. While the outer battle is vital and pressing, it cannot be fought as it should be unless the Christian is successfully winning the war *within*. Do you know how to fight the war within? This book—reflecting the spirit of the Word of God—has been written to tell you in no uncertain terms that there is a way to victory. And, avoiding the path of mere theory, it explains how you, no matter how many times you have been defeated in the past, can begin to consistently win the battles within.